Dr.
Johnson's
Household

Dr. Johnson's Household

Lyle Larsen

Archon Books
1985

First published 1985 as an Archon Book,
an imprint of The Shoe String Press, Inc.
Hamden, Connecticut 06514

Printed in the United States of America

The paper in this book meets the guidelines for
permanence and durability of the Committee on
Production Guidelines for Book Longevity of the
Council on Library Resources.

Library of Congress Cataloging in Publication Data

Larsen, Lyle, 1942–
  Dr. Johnson's household.

  Bibliography: p.
  Includes index.
  1. Johnson, Samuel, 1709–1784—Biography.
2. Johnson, Samuel, 1709–1784—Friends and
associates.   3. Authors, English—18th century—
Biography.   4. London (England)—
Biography.   5. London (England)—Social life and
customs—18th century.   I. Title.   II. Title: Doctor
Johnson's household.
PR3533.L37   1985   828'.609 [B]   85–4056
ISBN 0–208–02078–0 (alk. paper)

To the proprietors of
Sam: Johnson's Bookshop
Los Angeles

Contents

The business of the biographer is often
to pass slightly over those performances and
incidents, which produce vulgar greatness,
to lead the thoughts into domestick privacies,
and display the minute details of daily life.

Rambler, No. 60

Preface

James Boswell's *Life of Samuel Johnson,* first published in 1791, had a powerful effect on me the first time I read it. It struck a soul-deep note that no previous book had done in quite the same way. Here was a volume more engrossing than any novel, with a main character as vivid as anything Dickens could create. Better still, the story was real, not fictitious.

Several years later I read the *Life* again, and this time I became interested in some of the more minor characters, particularly in that strange collection of people whom Johnson sheltered and cared for during the last part of his life, the assembly that Boswell called Dr. Johnson's *ménage.* This group included Francis Barber, Johnson's black servant, who was born a slave in Jamaica and was brought to England at the age of five; Anna Williams, the blind poetess; Elizabeth Desmoulins, the daughter of Johnson's godfather; Robert Levett, the lowly practitioner of physic; and Poll Carmichael, the "stupid slut" who was always "wiggle-waggle" and whom Johnson could never get to be categorical.

These people in Boswell's *Life* seemed to revolve around Johnson as ever-present but indistinct satellites. But exactly who were they, I wondered. Where did they come from? Of what significance were they to Johnson? Boswell had provided just enough information to pique my curiosity. I went on to read Sir John Hawkins's *Life of Samuel Johnson,* Mrs. Thrale's *Anecdotes of the late Samuel Johnson,* Fanny Burney's *Diaries,* Johnson's *Letters,* Boswell's *Journals,* and other works in which these people were always there, moving through the scenes of Johnson's life like walk-on players, performing their little stage business or delivering their few lines and then departing. The focus, of course, was always on Johnson, and those on the periphery of his life remained shadowy and undefined.

The more I searched the more I realized how little was known about these people. Much had been written about the "Johnson Circle," that remarkable group of acquaintances that included Boswell, Fanny Burney, Oliver Goldsmith, Edmund Burke, David Garrick, Sir Joshua Reynolds, and others. But no study existed of those poor people who lived with Johnson in daily intimacy, who shared his breakfast table, who brewed his tea, who served his dinner when guests were present, who prayed with him at night, who helped by their mere presence to lessen his terrors of loneliness, who often made his life miserable with their bickering, yet who received his continual affection and charity, often without gratitude. So far, this story has not been told; it is the purpose of this book, however, to explain who these people were, where they came from, and what role they played in Dr. Johnson's life, as well as to give some insights into the interpersonal relationships and the daily routine of the household in general.

In the case of Anna Williams, her early life is inextricably bound up with that of her father, and so a large part of her story is devoted to the tribulations of Zachariah Williams. Here it is more than just biographical events that make the father important in the life of the daughter; it is also a matter of family temperament. To understand the character of the peevish and often overbearing Anna, one must understand something about the strongwilled and eccentric Zachariah.

As for Samuel Johnson, he appears in this work more than I originally intended. This book, after all, was to be a study of the members of Johnson's household, not of Dr. Johnson himself. I soon realized, however, just how foolish it was to ignore Johnson's presence; Johnson *was* a member of the household—not just the cohesive element—but its very nucleus. Those things, therefore, that bear upon Johnson's "domestick privacies, and display the minute details of daily life" are freely discussed. The mere "performances and incidents" in Johnson's life "which produce vulgar greatness" and are familiar to those who are familiar with Boswell, are brought in only insofar as they supply chronology and cohesiveness to the narrative.

Here I wish to thank the following persons and institutions for their generous assistance in making this book possible: Gerald Barron, M.D., for information regarding the history and development of cataract surgery; Mary Hyde for permission to print Anna Williams's letter of 5 August 1772 to Mrs. Percy; Mr. Geoffrey Nicolle of Rosemarket, Wales, for material on the Williams family; Mr. J. Moss, Registrar and Clerk to the Governors, Charterhouse, London, for information on Zachariah Williams's residence in the Charterhouse; the National Portrait Gallery for permission to use the photograph of Samuel Johnson's death mask; and Dr. John J. McManmon of Indiana University of Pennsylvania and my good friend Robert Klein for reading the typescript and suggesting many useful changes and revisions.

1   Anna and Zachariah Williams

The history of Dr. Johnson's household actually begins in a small square in London about the time of Mrs. Johnson's death in 1752. But the history of the household is largely a story of its people, and so our narrative must commence some years before that, many miles distant from the dirty and soot-begrimed capital. We begin in Haverfordwest in the county of Pembrokeshire, Wales. From here the countryside rolls out in all directions in undulating hills of pasture land and grain fields. Beneath the town flows the Western Cleddau River, spanned by two stone bridges. Looking up from the bank, one can see the ancient castle-keep, all that remains of the fortress built by Gilbert de Clare in the twelfth century.

On the east bank of the river stand the ancient parish church of St. David and the ruins of Maurice de Prendergast's large twelfth century mansion. Some little distance to the south are the crumbled remains of Haroldstone, once the seat of the powerful Perrot family, and five miles to the northwest is the village of Rosemarket where in 1706 was born Anna Williams, the oldest member of Dr. Johnson's household.[1]

Nothing is known of Anna's mother except her name, Martha, and that she lived until at least 1714 when Anna was eight years old. Still, Anna is not known to have spoken of her.

Anna's father, Zachariah Williams, was a doctor; at least he passed for one in that lovely region far from big cities with their hospitals and university-trained physicians. Although he lacked formal medical training, he was a skilled and devoted amateur, and anyone suffering a broken leg or whooping cough was glad of his assistance. His neighbors regarded him as a learned man, and he had the reputation of being a Hebrew scholar.[2]

Energy and ambition were the hallmarks of Zachariah's character. Elaborate schemes to get money and plans for making mechanical inventions continually occupied his mind. Among his many cherished creations was a machine to be used aboard ships at sea to extract the salt from ocean water, thereby making it drinkable. But its time had not come, and the invention (whatever its real merit) was ignored. Working on another get-rich scheme, Zachariah sought a twenty-one-year lease to dig coal in the parish of Llangunnor, Carmarthenshire, but that, too, came to nothing. Finally, he embarked upon a scheme that was to alter and consume the remainder of his long life. It was a scheme that promised fame and riches but brought only frustration and grief to him and his daughter both.

This profound change in the lives of Zachariah and Anna Williams was initiated by an act of Parliament. Britain was now surveying the vast horizon, preparatory to building her mighty empire, and this depended on mastery of the seas. During the previous century, many advances had been made in the science of marine navigation, but one important aspect remained elusive—accurately determining longitude.

Figuring out latitude—the distance of any point between the equator and the pole—was relatively easy. The navigator simply had to measure the height of the sun, at its zenith, above the distant horizon. For this he used a sextant, an instrument something like a pair of compasses in which one leg is pointed at the horizon and the other leg pointed toward the sun. Taking into account the time of the year (that is to say, the shifting of the earth on its axis), the degree of angle between the sun and the horizon told the navigator his own position, north or south, in relationship to the pole and the equator.

Determining longitude—the position of any object from a given point, or meridian, east or west—was not so easy. Due to the rotation of the earth, there are no fixed reference points from which to measure. All that a seaman could rely on was "dead reckoning"—his ability to steer an accurate course by the magnetic compass, taking into account his speed, and calculating drift and leeway according to the trim of his ship. This was a difficult procedure under the best of conditions, but during foul weather and rough seas, it became almost impossible; a ship might be hundreds of miles off course with no way of discovering the fact until it ran aground on unsuspected rocks or an unfamiliar coast.

An accurate method of determining longitude would not only make navigation less hazardous, it would also greatly aid commerce, exploration, and naval strategy through more precise charting of positions at sea. Anxious to push ahead of her European rivals in dominating the seaways, Britain tried stimulating the inventiveness of her subjects; in 1713 Parliament offered rewards of £10,000, £15,000, and £20,000 to anyone who could devise a way of determining longitude at sea to within sixty, forty, and thirty geographical miles respectively.[3]

Many speculators and inventors submitted their various methods and devices, hoping to get a share of the reward. One of the most promising claimants was John Harrison of Barrow-upon-Humber in Lincolnshire. Harrison realized that determining a ship's east or west position on a rotating globe was a matter of measuring *time*, not actual distance. If a navigator knew the exact time of some given spot on the earth, say the observatory at Greenwich, England, and also the exact local time where he was, the difference in times would indicate how far east or west he was of that given spot. For this, a precise and reliable watch was needed, something that could be depended on to keep accurate time for months together in diverse weather conditions. No watch that precise had yet been developed. But in 1728 Harrison came to London with drawings for a "timekeeper" that he expected would meet the requirements set forth by the parliamentary act.

Over the next thirty-one years he perfected his "timekeeper," or chronometer, so that it was accurate to within ten miles, one-third the required distance, but the board overseeing the matter was reluctant to hand out any of the promised money, granting Harrison only scant installments from time to time and insisting on more and more tests of the instrument. Harrison petitioned Parliament. He complained that he was being subjected to frivolous trials and delays. More years passed. It was only after the king himself interposed that Parliament finally granted Harrison the full amount due him— this in 1773, only three years before his death.

Zachariah Williams, a year before Harrison came to London, supposed that he himself had made the breakthrough in solving the longitude problem. Other speculators, he said, were engaged in schemes of "fruitless Ingenuity." He insisted that the attempt to develop an accurate and precise chronometer was doomed to failure for many reasons, "the Obstruction of Movements by Friction, the Waste of their Parts by Attrition, the various Pressure of the Atmosphere, the Effects of different Effluvia upon Metals, the Power of Heat and Cold upon all Matter, the Changes of Gravitation and the Hazard of Concussion."[4] He also rejected lunar charts, which attempted to calculate position by the motions of the moon.

His own method relied on the magnetic compass. It had long been known that the magnetic needle, for some unknown reason, did not always point true north. Zachariah conceived that this variation was uniform and consistent, that variations in the needle were equal, at equal distances, east and west. Although the details of this theory still needed to be worked out, he was confident that his fortune was made, so he gave up his medical practice in Wales, packed his possessions, and in 1727, along with his daughter, set out for London.

Anna arrived in the great metropolis with considerable advantages. At twenty-one years of age she was good with her needle, animated in spirits, and easy of conversation. She wrote poetry, possessed a good understanding of scientific theory and principles, was genuinely conversant with books, and knew both French and Italian. London offered numerous attractions for the curious and intelligent stranger, and Anna desired to see them all.

Vauxhall, for example, across the Thames River from Pimlico, was just such a place. It was one of London's most famous pleasure gardens. For a shilling one gained entrance to the garden which stood behind an enclosure of trees and tall hedges. The grounds within were laid out in long straight gravel paths leading through groves and skirting pavilions, that brought one up to majestic porticoes, rotundas, and elaborately filigreed colonnades. The eye was continually delighted by the classical elegance of pillars, alcoves, grottoes, statues, and paintings, all tastefully displayed at suitable intervals throughout the grounds. At night all was illuminated by countless red, blue, green, and yellow lamps—some arranged in the forms of sun, stars, and constellations. Guests were often treated to fireworks, and under a great domed Gothic structure an orchestra played, wafting its music to all parts of the gardens.[5] Such refined urban pleasures seemed strange and wonderful for a young woman familiar with only the rugged scenes of Wales.

Farther up river stood Ranelagh, the other famous pleasure garden. It generally catered to a higher stratum of society. Here one expected to see dukes and duchesses among the highly fashionable. Also for a shilling, one could roam the corridors of Bedlam and watch the strange antics of the mentally deranged. Although the British Museum was not yet open to the public, many private museums, such as John Hunter's anatomical collection, attracted visitors. Anna missed little of what London offered in the way of instruction or harmless amusement.

Zachariah, meanwhile, ranged through the city trying to gain attention for his scheme. He soon grew acquainted with a number of gentlemen and set his proposals before them. Sufficiently impressed by what they saw, they offered Williams a joint subsidy during the time required to perfect his mathematical computations, the money to be repaid out of the parliamentary reward. His supporters also took his plans to the Lords Commissioners of the Admiralty. Lord Torrington thought the system promising enough that he pressured the board of commissioners in charge of the longitude matter to lay Zachariah's tables of calculations before no less an authority than Sir Isaac Newton. Newton, however, excused himself from evaluating the plans, protesting that he was too old; yet he casually observed that the plans were probably visionary anyway.

The job of evaluation then fell to Samuel Molineux, one of the Lords Commissioners of the Admiralty, "who engaged in it," said Zachariah, "with no great Inclination to favour me."[6] Molineux was working on his own longitude scheme, and when one of Zachariah's instruments caught his fancy, he had it copied surreptitiously on paper and then set about having a duplicate made for himself. Zachariah learned of this and altercations followed. They did not continue long, however, for Molineux soon died, and Zachariah's scheme was forgotten by the board.

At about this time Edmund Halley was at the peak of his brilliant career. In 1682 he had predicted the return of the comet that now bears his name. In addition to this, he had discovered a method of figuring the sun's parallax and was responsible for publishing Newton's *Principia Mathematica*. Williams made Halley's acquaintance through mutual friends, then placed the longitude papers in his hands, asking his opinion. Halley considered the plans for several weeks and then advised Williams to publish them, saying they would do infinite service to mankind. Beyond this bit of encouragement he could do nothing more.

Still, with the aid of his friends, Zachariah managed to get a hearing before the august Royal Society. A paper was read explaining his system, accompanied by a demonstration using a compass mounted upon an iron sphere to show variations observable in the magnetic needle. The Society gave their thanks and requested Williams to deposit his theory "properly sealed and attested among their Archives, for the information of Posterity."[7]

Zachariah was gratified by these attentions, but they fell short of his once splendid dream—the dream of coming to London, presenting his discoveries to the proper authorities, collecting his money, and basking in the fame that would surely follow. It had seemed so easy. Yet he was getting nowhere, and now he had to face reality. Reality told him that he was penniless. Only the charity of friends had supported him thus far, and that could not go on, especially since all avenues of hope had turned out dead ends and no better prospects seemed in the offing. He was also getting old, approaching sixty, with no ready means of turning a livelihood. But his straightforwardness, honesty, and belief in himself had always gained him friends willing to help in a scrape, and he was not disappointed now. He entered what he called "a period of retirement." With the aid of Sir John Philips of the Picton Castle Philipses in Wales, and upon the nomination of Sir Robert Walpole (a cousin by marriage of Sir John Philips), Zachariah was admitted on 29 September 1729 as a pensioner of the Charterhouse in Clerkenwell, London.

The Charterhouse was originally founded in the fourteenth century for a monastic order of Carthusian monks by Sir Walter Manny and the bishop of London, Michael de Northburgh. Henry VIII suppressed it in 1547. Later, the earls of Rutland built their town house on part of the grounds. In 1611 Thomas Sutton bought the property as an almshouse for elderly, destitute gentlemen and as a school for poor boys. The school eventually moved to Godalming and St. Bartholomew's Medical School took its place; but that part of the ancient monastery buildings which housed and cared for old men, carries on its work to the present day.[8]

Zachariah was given a small room (No. 6), in the Charterhouse, took his meals in the common dining hall, and drew an annual allowance of £26.12s., paid in quarterly installments. He regarded his stay more as a hiatus in his career than as the closing chapter in a pathetic tale of ambition turned failure. Yet the Charterhouse was not the "safe and comfortable harbour for gentlemen of ship-wrecked fortunes" that he expected.[9] Instead, he found it "a den of thieves! the master a tyrannical oppressor; the servants fraudulent managers," and all the good intentions of the founder greatly abused and perverted.[10] The meals in the dining hall usually consisted of small portions of salted, ill-cooked beef without any sauce or vegetables, and small beer so watery as to be nearly tasteless.[11] The men who were confined to their chilly rooms by either sickness or old age received from the house only half a bushel of coal per week. Any extra had to be paid from their own pockets. Furthermore, it cost them an additional three pence a bushel to have the coal carried to their rooms. The nurses would not attend the sick without being paid, and, although a physician was kept by the house on a fixed salary, he, like the nurses, would do nothing without a fee. Not even toilets were provided by the house. The men had to provide their own or do without. When one of the pensioners died, his friends or relations had but two days to claim the body or else it was unceremoniously dumped into a hole and covered over. His belongings were then divided up among the house officials.

Zachariah openly criticized this state of affairs, and his outspokenness earned him the animosity of the staff and officials. He became a constant troublemaker, a thorn in the flesh, always complaining about something. He wrote to General James Oglethorpe, the noted philanthropist, who as a member of Parliament was instrumental in bringing about prison reform. Zachariah wanted him to seek a parliamentary inquiry into the operation of charitable institutions, particularly the Charterhouse, which might then result in the establishment of a code of standards to govern such charities. But Oglethorpe already had his hands full of business and was unwilling to take on more.

Despite the hostility and bickering that often passed between him and the Charterhouse staff, Zachariah managed to carry on with his studies into the longitude. During these years his daughter, Anna, with her keen mind and avid curiosity, called on him often, taking delight and interest in the progress of his work.

Among the other Charterhouse pensioners was Stephen Gray,

an experimenter like Zachariah Williams. The two men often spent long hours together lost in scientific talk. Gray was one of the early investigators of electricity. He had discovered, for example, that electricity could be transmitted from one substance to another and that some materials are excellent conductors. To demonstrate this, he payed out a length of packthread through which, by means of a charged glass rod, he sent a current the distance of 870 yards; this was the world's first electric line. He further discovered that it was not necessary to have contact to pass an electrical current, a phenomenon known as induction. He noted that water could be used as a conductor and that resin was a good insulator. For these discoveries the Royal Society awarded him the gold Copley medal. Later, in 1735, he succeeded in producing an electric spark by bringing a charged glass rod into contact with a metal bar resting on bands of silk. Fascinated by these experiments, Anna began assisting Gray in his work, and it was she who first observed the passing of an electric spark from the human body. She was proud of this distinction, and she remembered the event all of her life, not only because of the exciting, pioneering aspect of it, but because it was the last memorable event of her life before she went blind.

The state of her vision had alarmed her for some time. It seemed to be weakening. As the months passed, her sight grew progressively dimmer until the nature of the disorder became apparent: it was cataracts. The disease seldom afflicts people under fifty years of age, yet Anna was little more than thirty, with cataracts in both eyes. Her vision grew rapidly worse, and by 1740 she was totally blind. The calamity was hard to bear, yet Anna, like her father, refused to be undone by adversity. She carried on with life as before, without complaint, as much as her disability and poverty allowed. Her needle still brought in a small income, and with the help of friends who read to her, she continued her studies.

Zachariah went on with his researches. Finally, as Edmund Halley had urged many years before, he published in 1740, at his own expense, a pamphlet of forty-one pages, set up in large type, explaining his method of ascertaining the longitude. Five years later he brought out a second edition, the original portion being revised, with another forty-seven pages added to it. The work bore a long, explanatory title, typical of an earlier age:

The Mariners Compass Compleated: or, The Complement

of the Art of Navigation Discover'd and Propos'd. Being a Dissertation concerning the *Magnetical Variations* of the Mariners Compass, and the Variation of that same Variation, (according to a new Hypothesis and System.) As Also Directions for the Use of an *Universal Instrument*, Invented for Ready Knowing the Variations of the Mariners Compass, *at all Times and Places*.

By 1745 Zachariah had reached his seventies, and his health began to decline. He suffered pains in the kidneys and periodic convulsive attacks. The illness grew so debilitating that by October he could not leave his room. The nurses and other attendants gave him no assistance and only added to his problems. They refused to perform customary chores: they would not bring him food, make his bed, or light the fire in the grate; nor would they wash his bedsheets, shirts, or towels. He was told that he might have these things done if he hired some of them by the quarter, but he could not afford the expense. The bed eventually grew so foul that he had to sleep on the floor, which further aggravated his illness. As a result, Miss Williams, despite her blindness and poverty, had to come from her lodgings in the City to care for her father. By the summer of 1746 he was so much weakened by his sickness, compounded by neglect on the part of the Charterhouse staff, that he could not stir from his bed. Anna spent days, sometimes weeks at a stretch tending him, though she could do very little beyond providing the essentials for cleanliness and survival.

The servants resented Miss Williams's intrusion and her thwarting of their attempts at petty extortion, but they worked her presence to their advantage. They spread word that she was living in the same room with her father, knowing that it was against the rules for a woman to reside within the walls of the Charterhouse. It was even hinted that Miss Williams was not Zachariah's daughter—that a more sinister relationship existed between them. The rumors eventually had the desired effect.

Ever since his confinement, Zachariah had been given an added allowance of six shillings a week in lieu of the meals he missed in the common dining hall, plus an extra half bushel of coal. These courtesies, together with the usual allowance due him, suddenly stopped. The Williamses knew nothing of the evil rumors being spread; they realized only that their situation had suddenly become critical.

Anna called on the master of the Charterhouse, Nicholas Mann, graduate of King's College, Cambridge, and an excellent scholar.[12] In speaking with him she intended three things: to acquaint him with her father's dismal condition, to inform him of the understaff's gross negligence, and to find out what had happened to her father's allowance. She began the interview diplomatically by thanking Mann for his indulgence in first granting her father the additional pittance of money and coal. Yet, before she got very far, Mann blurted out that he had no intention of listening to her, that he had reasons for what he did, and that Zachariah Williams could complain to the board of governors if he pleased. Anna was astonished by this sudden outburst, not knowing what had provoked it.

Less than a fortnight later the mystery was cleared up when Mr. Pike, the sexton and housekeeper, and Mr. Reyner, another pensioner and usher of the halls, came into Zachariah's room. They carried a message from Mr. Mann that Zachariah's former allowance and provision of coal would be stopped so long as Miss Williams disobeyed the rules and remained in the Charterhouse. When they asked to know what Mr. Williams had to say to this, Zachariah replied that since he was unable to help himself, the master must do his pleasure by him. The messengers thought this not a sufficient answer and pressed him for a better. Unable to restrain herself any longer, Anna broke in, saying,

> Pray, my compliments to Mr. Mann, and tell him I should take it as a favour if he'd condescend at a leisure hour to call and see what an infirm state and condition my father is in, and that whenever the Master should appoint a person to attend and take proper care of my father, both night and day, as his case requires, I will instantly quit the place, but not till then.[13]

Mann sent no further word. He thought it better in dealing with such recalcitrants to starve them into compliance with the regulations. The injunction on Zachariah's allowance, therefore, continued, while the appalling conditions in his room grew worse. Winter's cold was fast approaching, and they had no coal for the fire except what Anna could bring in now and then from outside. Food was also hard to obtain. Meanwhile, the servants taunted and teased the pair, and whenever a friend came from outside to visit or to bring some necessary item, he was saluted with curses and insults.

The only pleasant event of the year was Anna's publication of a book, *The Life of the Emperor Julian*, a translation from the French of F. La Bleterie, which she made with the assistance of two sisters named Wilkinson. The book was not popular, however, and produced little income.

With conditions every day growing worse, something had to be done. In August, Anna wrote a polite yet plainspoken letter to Mann. "It is with great Reluctance I am obliged to undertake a Task which I already fear will prove too hard for me to perform without shewing a Resentment," the letter began.[14] She then enumerated the injustices done her father, calling upon Mann to redress them. The letter went unanswered.

On the first of October she wrote again. Once more she cited the harsh treatment shown her father, especially the sudden termination of his allowance. "What could induce one, whose universal Character is Goodness and Humanity, to act such a Part?—I can't any way account for!" What crime must her father have committed, she wanted to know, to deserve such punishment? "But for my Assistance, and that of other private Friends, he must inevitably had died for Want, in the midst of one of the noblest Charities in the known World!"[15] Mann still remained silent.

In a letter dated the 12th of October, Anna appealed to Lord Chancellor Hardwicke, a governor of the Charterhouse, recounting the deplorable conditions of her father's case. She also stated that she had written to Mr. Mann but had received no response.[16] Hardwicke, some weeks later, wrote to Sir John Philips, the man who originally got Williams admitted to the Charterhouse, saying that he would do all in his power to get Zachariah justice. The Williamses heard of this and were encouraged.

In December, with the help of Anna, Zachariah drafted a petition to all the governors of the Charterhouse. He stated his complaints, emphasizing that he would surely have perished were it not for his daughter's help.[17] He wished to stress the necessity of Anna's care as a defense for transgressing the rule against allowing women to live in the Charterhouse. In the address preceding the petition, he asked for permission to retire into the country for benefit of the air.

When this petition produced no results, a second one, an exact copy of the first, was sent to the board the following February 1747. On the 18th the governors met and brought Zachariah before them to hear his complaints. No notice was taken of his petition. Unfortunately, he was extremely ill, even delirious; he could neither comprehend nor answer the questions put to him. He had with him, however, a written account of his case which he tried to get read, but it was not allowed, and he was carried back to his room nearly senseless.

Four months dragged by with no further steps being taken. Zachariah had at least got through the winter, and the coming of spring slightly eased the oppressive conditions in which he lived.

Another meeting of the governors was scheduled for midsummer. On the third of June, Anna again wrote to Lord Chancellor Hardwicke reminding him of his promise of justice to her father. She further mentioned that she knew the board was to meet on the following day "where I earnestly intreat your Lordship would be pleased to move that an Enquiry be made into the Case of that poor oppressed Petitioner."[18] She also wrote to another of the governors, Lord Chief Justice Willes, acquainting him with the situation of her father, "who, on strict Enquiry made, will be found to have met with very unequitable Treatment from Mr. Mann, the Master of the *Charter-House*, and his Accomplices, whether wilfully or ignorantly I won't presume to determine."[19]

The meeting had to be postponed, but the governors finally met on the 24th. Anna sat outside the meeting room hoping to be called. The governors heard Zachariah's petition, then reviewed the order of 1731 which forbade lodging women in the Charterhouse. Next, Mann came forward to testify that Williams had kept his daughter in his room for nearly two years against repeated admonitions. One of Anna's letters to him was also read. Zachariah, meanwhile, feeling stronger than when he was carried before the board four months earlier, waited in his room, prepared this time to present his case to the board. The points that he wished to cover were carefully written out on a sheet of paper. But the board did not choose to see him, and promptly it issued an order that Anna Williams should quit the Charterhouse and that no allowance be given Zachariah till she had.[20] This action further entrenched both parties and placed them at irreconcilable odds—the governors determined that the rules be obeyed, Anna Williams equally determined not to budge until her father received decent attention and proper medical care. And so matters stood for eight months.

On 13 February 1748 the governors once more admonished Zachariah for violating house rules, but the Williamses stood firm. Then on May 9th the governors met again. This time they issued an order announcing that "for his repeated and continued Disobedience to the Orders of the Governors the said Zachariah Williams be expelled the Hospital."[21] The ultimatum was brought to Zachariah the following Friday evening while Anna was away. Next morning several of the staff came into his room. He was weak and unable to sit up in his bed. They taunted him, insulted him, pulled off his blankets, and dragged him onto the floor. The next day they came back and once more pulled him out of bed.

Then early Monday morning, with the sanction of Mr. Mann, who now had the authority of the board's expulsion order behind him, they returned with a vengeance. Bursting into his room, they tumbled Zachariah to the floor, tore off the bedding, and dismantled the bed. "The Master may use his Pleasure by me," Zachariah told them, too weak to resist their rage; "I have been God's Prisoner in this Room these two Years and a half, and cannot help myself; take Care what you do."[22] They unhinged the doors, took out the shutters, and removed the windows. In their frenzy, they ripped up manuscripts, destroyed books, and shattered valuable mathematical instruments. Everything belonging to the apartment they carried off, leaving Zachariah helpless on the floor. He lay there all that day and night, and the next day until evening when some visitors noticed his state and gave him aid. Soon afterward he was carried out of the Charterhouse and placed in the care of a friend.

He and his daughter now found themselves in the lowest and most dismal condition of their lives—Anna, at forty-two, blind and impoverished; Zachariah, at seventy-five, almost dead.

2   Enter Samuel Johnson

With better food and greater care, Zachariah Williams slowly regained part of his health. The return of strength brought renewed ambition, and once again the longitude scheme rose uppermost in his mind. The prize money was still being offered, but it was now more than just money or reputation that drove him on; it was the pressure of time. He longed not to have the work of over thirty years descend with him into the grave. He looked around for someone with influence who would sponsor him. After approaching several important people without success, he encountered a man who wielded very little influence, but who made up for it with a sympathetic ear and at least a willingness to help. The man was Samuel Johnson.[1]

Johnson was then forty-two years old. His reputation at this time rested largely upon *London, a Poem; The Vanity of Human Wishes;* the dramatic tragedy *Irene;* and his "Plan," addressed to Lord Chesterfield, for a dictionary of the English language. The *Rambler* essays were only recently begun, and they were published anonymously.

Johnson took Zachariah Williams home with him, and as he loved mathematical calculations and was easily enthralled by the workings of machinery, Johnson listened attentively as Williams explained his tables of computations and demonstrated his theories on instruments of his own making. The system appeared sound, but what appealed most to Johnson was the old speculator himself—a man nearly eighty years old, poverty-ridden, shabbily clothed; but a man with purpose, determination, and vigor.

Besides discussing his theories and inventions, Williams spoke freely of his personal hardships—the years of disappointment trying to gain a fair hearing for his longitude discoveries, the years of neglect and virtual imprisonment in the Charterhouse. The only kind words he voiced were for several friends and especially his daughter. She, too, had suffered much, particularly the loss of her sight, but she seldom complained. Williams praised her talents, unselfishness, and piety so warmly that Johnson's wife, overhearing what he said, expressed a strong desire to meet this remarkable woman. Consequently, Zachariah brought his daughter by. The Johnsons, when they met her, were pleased to find a plainly though meticulously dressed woman, exceedingly proper, with a clear, pleasant voice, and a sensible store of conversation. The women liked one another immediately. Although Mrs. Johnson was eighteen years older than Anna, the women had several things in common: both were strongwilled and intelligent, and both appreciated literature. As Johnson was busy most of the day with his writing and studies, Mrs. Johnson offered Miss Williams an invitation to call whenever she liked.

The work that engaged Johnson most of the day was his dictionary. The project was conceived in 1746 and begun in 1748. It went forward in good earnest the following year when he took his present house in Gough Square. The garret was fitted up as a workroom where six assistants were employed. Desks were set up for them to work at so that the place looked like the bookkeeping room of some business establishment. Scraps of paper littered the floor. Books lay strewn about. Some were stacked up in corners.

The work progressed in a fairly set routine: Johnson perused those English authors whose use of the language he considered the purest and most correct. When he found a word or construction he wished to include in his dictionary, he underlined it, wrote the initial letter in the margin, and drew two vertical lines alongside the sentence in which it occurred. The books were then turned over to the amanuenses. They copied each sentence onto a separate slip of paper and filed it alphabetically with the other words collected. Later Johnson furnished definitions from his own head and supplied etymologies from other writers on the subject.[2] It was a gigantic task and its progress seemed dishearteningly slow, yet Johnson found the even pace and set ritual not altogether unpleasant.

With all this work, Johnson still found time to help Anna and Zachariah Williams. First of all, he encouraged Anna's literary ambitions. She entertained the idea of bringing together a miscellaneous collection of her poems and some essays, and Johnson wrote for her "Proposals for printing, by subscription, Essays in Verse and

Prose, by Anna Williams." This appeared in the September issue of the *Gentleman's Magazine* (see Appendix A).

Furthermore, Anna had in her possession a letter which supposedly came from the pen of Sir Walter Raleigh, and Johnson agreed that if it was authentic, she might get some money by publishing it. He sent the manuscript to Thomas Birch, who was then preparing a new edition of Raleigh's works. He requested that Birch inspect it, saying,

> I perceive no proofs of forgery in my examination of it, and the Owner tells me that, as he [*sic*] has heard, the handwriting is Sir Walter's. If you should find reason to conclude it genuine, it will be a kindness to the owner, a blind person, to recommend it to the Booksellers.[3]

The letter, it seems, turned out a counterfeit, and so the plan fell through.

The following year, 1751, Zachariah got Johnson's help in writing letters to several lords of the Admiralty, requesting a further hearing for his longitude scheme. Months of delay followed, due in part to Zachariah's precarious health; but finally the plans were inspected by Dr. James Bradley, the Astronomer Royal. Bradley was shown a page of tables and a "magnetical globe," simulating the earth, on which were marked the variations in compass reading at any given latitude and longitude. Zachariah claimed that he could instantly calculate on this instrument the exact longitude if he was only given the year, latitude, and compass variation. Wary, however, of having his work again purloined, he concealed from Bradley the principles on which the tables were made and would not allow him to see the inner construction of the globe. Bradley complained of this in his report to the Board. He added that whereas Zachariah's calculations often closely agreed with the best observations of others, in several instances the difference was so great that he did not think the system could be relied on at sea.[4]

This year also witnessed a marked decline in the health of Johnson's wife. As early as 1748 Elizabeth (or "Tetty" as her husband affectionately called her) rented a room in a small house beyond the church at Hampstead, about four miles from the city; here she retired occasionally for the sake of better air.[5] As a young woman, living in Birmingham, some twelve miles from Johnson's Lichfield, she had

possessed attractive features: a fair complexion; a small, somewhat
coquetish mouth; dark blue eyes; a high, dignified forehead; and
wheat-colored hair. She married Henry Porter, a woolen draper of
Birmingham, about 1714 and bore him two sons and a daughter.
Porter died in 1734, and the following year, against the wishes of her
sons, Elizabeth married Sam Johnson. She was nearly twice his age—
he twenty-six and she forty-six. Now, sixteen years later, Tetty was
fat. She caked her puffy cheeks with rouge and would have dyed her
hair black had not Johnson absolutely forbidden it. Being descended
from an ancient family, now with little money or position, she delighted in buying herself fine things—some lace here, a pair of gloves
there—and occasionally ran up small debts that Johnson could not
pay.

People noticed a slight affectation of gentility in her speech and
behavior. David Garrick, who had known the couple since early Lichfield days, considered her no more than a little painted puppet. Some
thought her a hypochondriac because Hampstead, with its mineral
spring waters, was the resort not only of illness, but also of pleasure;
and when Tetty was not in bed reading romances and nursing herself
with large quantities of liqueur and opium, she was seen indulging
in "nice living, at an unsuitable expense, while her husband was
drudging in the smoke of London."[6] Opium was widely used at the
time, of course, as a medicine for almost any ailment; it furnished
quick relief from nearly all pain either of body or mind. The liqueur
helped Tetty to reconcile the reality of her life, commonplace and
unprosperous, with her dreams of life as it ought to be, refined and
affluent.

In order not to be alone at Hampstead, Tetty lived with a longtime Midlands friend, Elizabeth Swynfen, a woman in her early thir-
ties, who would later become the Mrs. Desmoulins of Johnson's
household. Miss Swynfen's father, Samuel Swynfen, had begun practice as a surgeon in Lichfield. At the age of twenty-seven, in 1709,
he was lodging in the house of Michael Johnson, the bookseller, when
the latter's eldest son was born.[7] He thus became Samuel Johnson's
godfather and gave to him his name. A year later, in 1710, Dr. Swynfen
married Mabella Fretwell of Hallaby, Yorkshire, and between the years
1711 and 1727, they had eleven children. Elizabeth was born in 1716,
and like the other children, she was baptized at Lichfield Cathedral.
Sometime in the mid-1720s, Dr. Swynfen moved his family to Bir-

mingham where the city's larger population promised a more substantial practice than could be had in the small cathedral town. It was in Birmingham that Tetty (then Elizabeth Porter) met Miss Swynfen, and it was through the Swynfen family that she was later introduced to Samuel Johnson.

When Johnson came out to Hampstead to visit his wife, which he did whenever he could get away from his work in the city, he took another room in the same house; here he wrote *The Vanity of Human Wishes*. Due to her illness (real or imagined), her age (she was nearly sixty), or simply disinterest, Tetty no longer countenanced physical intimacy with her husband. She sometimes allowed a visiting female friend to share her bed, but only on a promise not to tell anyone; she did not wish her husband to learn that she granted to others the company that she denied to him on the grounds of ill health.[8] Being a man of strong sexual desires, this deprivation proved a great strain, and Miss Swynfen, whom he had known all of her life, increasingly gained more of his attention. She was not particularly attractive, nor intellectually gifted, but she became a growing source of temptation. Part of her domestic duties was to warm Johnson's bed late at night with a pan of coals. When she was finished and had departed, Johnson would quickly undress, get into bed, then call her back to him. She would sit on the edge of the bed talking, Johnson stroking her back; then he would slowly draw her down till she lay at full length on the bed with her head on his pillow. The petting and fondling continued until Johnson could stand it no longer; his moral sense would not let him proceed: suddenly he would cry out in anguish and push her from him.[9] Not that his wife, sleeping in the next room, cared what he did. She had earnestly told him that he might lie with as many women as he pleased so long as he loved only her. But Johnson possessed a severe and punishing conscience that his appetite, strong as it was, could not overthrow.

When Tetty began rapidly losing weight and the color in her face vanished, it was apparent that her complaints were genuine and that she was really ill. Her sickness brought her and Miss Williams into closer friendship than ever, for now they had one more thing in common—they could commiserate over each other's physical condition.

Johnson made his wife as comfortable as possible and provided for her as best he could. He also pondered what could be done for

Miss Williams, for it seemed likely that an operation might restore her sight. He broached the subject to John Hawkins, who was a friend of Samuel Sharp, senior surgeon of Guy's Hospital and the foremost authority in England on cataract surgery.[10] Johnson wanted Hawkins to use his influence to find out what might be arranged to help Miss Williams. As Hawkins, too, admired the woman's indomitable spirit, her intelligence, and, above all, her piety, he readily consented. He went to Sharp and laid Miss Williams's case before him; he spoke of her abilities and her character, and he explained that she was too poor to afford regular medical attention. Sharp was moved by this appeal, and he agreed to perform the necessary operation free of charge. Since the room where Miss Williams lodged was so cramped, arrangements were made for her to move presently into the Johnson house. Here the operation could be performed more conveniently and she could convalesce in much greater comfort.

For two years now Johnson had been writing his *Rambler* essays. They appeared every Tuesday and Saturday. As Tetty's health worsened, she gave up her room in Hampstead and moved back to Gough Square, where the strain on Johnson made semiweekly publication too oppressive. Consequently, in mid-March of 1752, the essays came to an abrupt end. "Time, which puts an end to all human pleasures and sorrow, has likewise concluded the labours of the Rambler," he wrote in the last issue. "The reasons of this resolution it is of little importance to declare...." Although highly regarded, the essays were not widely popular; they were too grave and philosophical to excite much common interest. "I am far from supposing," Johnson continued in this last paper, "that the cessation of my performances will raise any enquiry, for I have never been much a favourite of the publick...."[11] Nevertheless, choice passages— passages with more popular appeal—were excerpted to appear in other periodicals such as the monthly *Gentleman's Magazine*.

Tetty was soon advised to sleep out of town that she might gain some benefit from cleaner air. "When she was carried to the lodgings that had been prepared for her," Johnson recalled years later, "she complained that the staircase was in very bad condition, for the plaster was beaten off the walls in many places. 'Oh,' said the man of the house, 'that's nothing but by the knocks against it of the coffins of the poor souls that have died in the lodgings!'"[12]

Tetty always appreciated her husband's writing, and in the early days of their marriage, when he was struggling to make a name in the world, that support meant a great deal to him. She particularly liked the *Rambler* essays. "I thought very well of you before," she told him when the papers first began appearing, "but I did not imagine you could have written any thing equal to this."[13] Now, as she lay critically ill in a strange house, Johnson presented her with the first collected edition of the essays, in four volumes, just published by Payne and Bouquet. In the third volume he inscribed, "Eliz. Johnson, March 13th 1752." The gift came just in time. Four days later Tetty died.

Johnson received word at Gough Square late in the evening of the 17th. Immediately he wrote in anguish to his friend the Reverend Doctor John Taylor. Johnson implored him to come at once. Taylor got the note at his home in Westminster at three in the morning, threw on his clothes, and hastened to Gough Square where he found Johnson weeping uncontrollably. Soon Johnson grew calm enough to ask Taylor to join with him in prayer, but the next day he was still greatly agitated and once more wrote to his friend: "Let me have your company and instruction. Do not live away from me. My distress is great."[14]

Tetty was buried several days later in the church of Bromley in Kent.

3 Francis Barber and No. 17 Gough Square

Our scene now briefly changes, and we travel four thousand miles southwest from England to the island of Jamaica, ninety miles east of Cuba, in the Caribbean Sea. Here we begin tracing the origins of Francis Barber, the longest standing member of Dr. Johnson's household.

Jamaica is approximately the size of Wales or the states of Connecticut and Rhode Island combined. It enjoys a tropical climate, white beaches, and fertile soil. During the seventeenth and eighteenth centuries, it harbored many lawless groups such as the buccaneers, who used the southern coast of the island as a base from which to ravage the growing shipping trade in the area. They operated virtually unmolested from atop the cliff city of Port Royal—virtually unmolested, that is, until the morning of 7 June 1692, when a tremendous earthquake dumped two-thirds of the city into the sea. The more law-abiding world said that it was divine retribution for Port Royal's extreme wickedness.[1]

In addition to the buccaneers, the island sheltered other pirates such as the brutal Edward Teach, better known as "Blackbeard." His hair hung down to his broad shoulders, and he is said to have woven into his thick, wiry black beard sulphurous fuses which he lit before going into battle to appear more fierce. There were also the suave but murderous "Calico Jack" Rackham and his two shipmates, the notorious women pirates, Mary Read and Anne Bonny.[2]

When the British, during the reign of Cromwell, seized control of Jamaica and ran the Spaniards out in 1655, many of the Spanish-owned black slaves fled into the mountainous interior of the island where they formed into loosely-molded communities. For nearly a century, as the European population grew, these tribes made periodic forays into the lowlands to steal cattle, provisions, tools, and whatever came to hand. Eventually, the descendants of these slaves, who down the line had interbred with what remained of a small native population, came to be known as "Maroons" or were simply referred to as "the wild men." Their raids became so damaging to the lowland British planters that regular army troops were dispatched from England. The Redcoats trudged after the wild men through mountain forests, occasionally engaging them in skirmishes which have since been dignified with the name of Maroon Wars.[3]

Agriculture on the island increased year by year, so to work the fields, more blacks were imported from Africa—about five thousand annually.[4] Many of these were from characteristically docile tribal cultures—mostly Iboes, along with some Mandingoes; but others were Whydahs and Coromantynes, more self-willed and aggressive peoples.[5] At times slave uprisings brought bloodshed, the most violent being Tacky's Rebellion in 1760 in which about sixty whites were slain and over three hundred blacks.[6] Yet despite these perils, many British subjects were willing to undertake the long Atlantic voyage to become West Indian planters. Europe was becoming increasingly hungry for sweetmeats and other sugar-made foods, and the climate of Jamaica was ideally suited to producing sugar cane. Therefore, even with pirates and wild men to contend with, vast fortunes could be amassed.

The Bathursts were among these early British planters. In 1674 King Charles II granted to John Bathurst 4,000 acres of land in the parish of St. Mary on the northern coast of the island.[7] Bathurst named the estate Orange River Plantation and began raising sugar cane. In the year of his death, 1701, in addition to the land itself, his property consisted of 20 mules and 30 steers, plus indentured servants and slaves to the number of 44 men and 53 women. These slaves bore typical slave names such as Cowtaile, Mercury, Scipio, Hamah Papa, Grand Tomba, Substance Sonny, and Tickle Pitcher.

John Bathurst's son, Richard, a native of England, County of Lincoln, inherited the plantation and ran it successfully for many years. He later obtained a commission in the Jamaica Militia for which he was then known locally as "Colonel." Unfortunately, as the years passed, poor management led to financial difficulties and soon Colonel Bathurst found himself deeply in debt with much of his land heavily mortgaged. By 1742 Orange River Plantation had shrunk from 4,000 to 2,000 acres. Heading steadily toward ruin, and unable to handle the worsening situation due to advancing age, Bathurst decided to sell. In August of 1749 he sold the plantation to William Lamb of Kingston for £12,800. The property conveyed in this transaction amounted to the entire 2,600 acres of land, all the muscovado sugar and rum that it contained, 143 slaves, 13 mules, 75 head of cattle, 50 cottages, several horses, and an unspecified number of goats, hogs, and poultry. The only property exempted from the sale were some slaves for whom Bathurst was particularly fond, one of them apparently Francis Barber.

The young black boy did not then, of course, have the aristocratic sounding English name by which he was known in Dr. Johnson's household; he did not get that until several months after the sale when Colonel Bathurst brought him into England. In Jamaica, for the first eight years of his life, he had a slave name. In later years Francis never talked about his Jamaican life, though he was old enough when he left to have remembered much of it—at least no recollections of his early years are recorded. Probably no one was interested in hearing them. We find what appears to be his Jamaican name, however, in the deed of sale between Bathurst and William Lamb. The document is catalogued as "Liber Old Series 137" and is kept in The Jamaica Archives at Spanish Town where it slowly decays from the tropical humidity. It is now almost too fragile to handle. Just above Bathurst's signature is a clause which excludes from the sale four slaves, including "a negro woman named Nancy," who was given her freedom, "and a negro boy named Quashey."[8] We know that Bathurst left the island soon after completing the sale of his property and that he took with him a slave boy, eight years old, whom, upon arriving in England in 1750, he had baptized and renamed Francis Barber. This Quashey is probably the same child. A family named Barber lived near Bathurst in Jamaica. It seems probable that Francis was named for this family or for a member of it.

We may know even more about Francis from a deed of sale entered two years earlier, on 23 September 1747. We learn the name of his mother, and we also learn that he was one of at least two boys in the family. This document records the "conveyance [to Bathurst] of a negro woman slave named Grace and her two children Luckey and Quashy. Consideration 5£ currency."[9]

Once in England, Colonel Bathurst went to live with his son, also named Richard, a doctor of physic in Lincoln. Francis was sent to the Reverend William Jackson's school in the distant hamlet of Barton, Yorkshire, to learn reading and writing.[10] He remained there for about two years, returning at the age of ten to act as servant to the young doctor. Dr. Bathurst had been a close friend of Samuel Johnson's for years, so close, in fact, that Johnson spoke of him years after his death as "*dear dear* Bathurst, whom I loved better than ever I loved any human creature."[11]

When Bathurst heard of Tetty's death in March of 1752, he knew that it would be cruel, and perhaps dangerous, to leave Johnson in a big house with only his imagination for companionship. Johnson's mind was naturally drawn to the morbid and terrifying aspects of existence, so that solitude for him was a horror; his fear amounted to a phobia, and he constantly went to great lengths not to be left by himself.[12] In these circumstances Bathurst perceived that Francis, with his cheerful disposition and gentle ways, might be just the thing to divert Johnson's melancholy thoughts. Francis would need Johnson's attention and guidance, being yet so young, and Francis, in turn, might be of service to Johnson in a number of useful ways. Accordingly, Bathurst packed Francis off to London where he arrived toward the end of March, about two weeks after Tetty's death.

He found the house to which he was sent tucked away in Gough Square, a quandrangle just off one of the busiest thoroughfares in the city. It is reached by any of four passages through a network of small courts and alleyways from the north side of Fleet Street. The building is No. 17, the big four-story dwelling on the west face of the square. Constructed of sturdy red brick, it was built about 1700 by a successful London tradesman. Johnson moved here from Holborn with his wife in 1749 to be closer to his publisher, William Strahan, who lived nearby at No. 10 Little New Street, Shoe Lane.

To the left, as Francis entered the front door, stood the dining room and on the right the parlor. In the basement, down a narrow, steep stair, was the kitchen with its two great fireplaces for cooking. The kitchen is where Francis, being a servant, would sleep. On the second floor were two more rooms: the withdrawing room to the left, and a bedroom to the right which Miss Williams now occupied. Two more bedrooms, one of them Johnson's, made up the third floor;

and above them was the long garret, the entire width of the house, where the dictionary was being compiled.

The mood throughout the house following Tetty's death continued mournful. Johnson went through the day half distracted with grief, going abroad in the evening to spend sleepless hours walking the midnight streets. Work on the dictionary stopped. He fell prey to morbid lethargy, and for over a month he could do nothing. Soon, however, he realized that despair was useless and that the best way to shake off the specters that haunted him was to immerse himself in work. "When my dear Mrs. Johnson expired," he told friends years later, "I sought relief in my studies, and strove to lose the recollection of her in the toils of literature."[13] In his notebook for May he entered a prayer which he had composed the month before, and under it he wrote, "I used this service, . . . May 6, as preparatory to my return to life to-morrow."[14]

With his return to the daily cares of living, he now regarded Francis with closer attention. The youngster's simplicity and good nature were endearing qualities, and his connection to the beloved Dr. Bathurst raised him all the more quickly in Johnson's affections. But Johnson had little need for a personal servant, so acting in the best interests of the boy, he put him to board at Mrs. Coxeter's so that he could attend nearby Blackfriar's School. Mrs. Coxeter was the daughter of Thomas Coxeter, who was known for his collection of old plays. When Thomas Coxeter died in 1747, leaving his daughter an orphan, Johnson had helped support her.[15]

Francis, however, attended school for only one day, for he came down with the smallpox. He was not a robust child to begin with. He was small for his age and slightly built, and he was easily susceptible to colds. Still, after recovering from the smallpox and returning to Gough Square, he was energetic enough to need more to occupy him than the trivial duties he was assigned, those of running errands and answering the door. Johnson again considered putting him in school, and this time he sent Francis to the Birmingham Free Grammar School to study under Mr. Desmoulins, writing master. Desmoulins (pronounced *Demullins*) had recently married Tetty's friend and Hampstead lodger, Miss Swynfen.

By this time Miss Williams was settled in the house, and all was in order for her cataract surgery; Sharp was ready to couch her.

Couching is an operation wherein the clouded lens of the eye is pushed back into the anterior chamber so that light can enter once again unobstructed. It was a relatively short but painful operation. The patient usually sat astride a bench facing the surgeon. The doctor held the patient's lower eyelid open with the fingers of his left hand while an assistant, standing behind the patient, held open the upper lid. The doctor cut into the side of the sclera, the white fibrous part of the eyeball, and into this half-inch wound inserted a needle with a spatula-shaped end. With the instrument between the lens and the iris, he pressed back on the lens until it broke free of the ligaments holding it in place, and continued pushing it down into the transparent, jelly-like vitreous humor that fills the eyeball. If the operation proved successful and no complications arose, the patient quickly recovered. He no longer had a lens to focus images onto the retina, but spectacles corrected that. Spectacles often made it possible for the patient to see well enough to read.[16]

Sharp's examination showed that Miss Williams had the worst type of cataract to deal with—it was a soft cataract, one that is "not ripe." In an essay on the subject a year later, Sharp described his procedure in a case similar to Miss Williams's.[17] On this occasion he made an incision in the patient's eye and inserted the needle to depress the lens, but the lens gave, and he was afraid that if he exerted any more force, he would evacuate all the vitreous humor. He then passed a little scoop into the eye and turned it several times, hoping to break the capsula which contained the lens, but the lens was too soft and yielding. He tried cutting the lens free with the point of his knife, but still he found not the least resistance. In such cases as this couching proved ineffectual, and blind Miss Williams must remain.

Johnson, meanwhile, had resumed drudging away at his dictionary, making slow but steady progress. Not far away his friend Samuel Richardson was publishing *The History of Sir Charles Grandison*, his third novel, following up the successes of *Pamela* and *Clarissa Harlowe*. Miss Williams loved the high moral tone of Richardson's works as much as did Johnson, and she wrote an adulatory poem titled "Verses to Mr. Richardson, on his History of Sir Charles Grandison" which Johnson showed the novelist. After praising each of the novels and their characters, the poem entreats the author to continue his lessons in how to "move the passions, and to mend the heart."

Thou sweet preceptor of the rising age,
Let still another work thy thoughts engage;
Proceed to teach, thy labours ne'er can tire,
Thou still must write, and we must still admire.[18]

Vanity being a prominent feature of Richardson's character, he was much taken by such effusive lines. He owned a publishing house in London, through which he published his own works, and he had the poem printed in a handsome quarto edition. This was not offered to the public for sale, but the poem appeared in the *Gentleman's Magazine* for January 1754. Richardson acknowledged his gratitude to Miss Williams by sending her a gift, probably the last volume of *Sir Charles Grandison*.[19]

Miss Williams believed the gift was genuine recognition of her artistic abilities, so she projected a greater undertaking: she envisioned putting together a dictionary of terms taken from natural philosophy and relating them to the conduct of everyday life. The tone of the work would attempt to cultivate in the reader a sense of piety and virtue. Hoping to profit from Richardson's prestige as a popular author and his position as publisher, she got Johnson to address her plan to him. "Sir," wrote Johnson on the 28th of March 1754,

> I am desired by Miss Williams, who has waited several times upon you without finding you at home, and has been hindered by an ilness [*sic*] of some weeks from repeating her visits, to return you her humble thanks for your present. She is likewise desirous to lay before you the inclosed plan which she has meditated a long time, and thinks herself able to execute by the help of an Amanuensis, having long since collected a great number of volumes on these subjects, which indeed she appears to me to understand better than any person that I have ever known. She will however want a few of the late books. She begs that if you think her dictionary likely to shift for itself in this age of dictionaries, you will be pleased to encourage her by taking some share of the copy, and using your influence with others to take the rest, or put her in any way of making the undertaking profitable to her. . . . She is certainly qualified for her work, as much as any one that will ever undertake it, as she

understands chimistry |sic| and many other arts with which
Ladies are seldom acquainted, and I shall endeavour to put
her and her helpmate into method. I can truly say that she
deserves all the encouragement that can be given her, for
a being more pure from any thing vicious I have never
known.[20]

Richardson, however, chose not to give Miss Williams more encouragement, so the plan died.

Zachariah, during all this time, kept trying to gain recognition
for his longitude scheme. Dr. Bradley's unfavorable report to the
Board had effectively killed any further hope of winning the parliamentary prize, but Zachariah was too stubborn to concede the fact.
Although above eighty years of age, with his body decayed and pal-
sied, his spirits remained little diminished. Johnson long before had
mastered the principles on which his theories were based, and to
aid him, he wrote a pamphlet titled "An Account of an Attempt to
Ascertain the Longitude at Sea, by an Exact Theory of the Variation
of the Magnetical Needle. With a Table of Variations at the most
remarkable Cities of Europe, from the Year 1660 to 1860 |sic|. By
Zachariah Williams." The pages on the right side, opposite the English text, carried an Italian translation by Joseph Baretti. This was
to disseminate the information over a wider area.

Johnson's name, meanwhile, was getting much better known. In
February of 1755 he received an honorary degree of Master of Arts
from Oxford University. This was to acknowledge the merit of his
Rambler essays, which the Chancellor of Oxford cited in his letter of
nomination as being "excellently calculated to form the manners of
the people, and in which the cause of religion and morality is every
where maintained by the strongest powers of argument and language."[21] The degree was also for the upcoming *Dictionary of the English
Language*, published three months later, in April, and already enlisting
praise from many of the learned.

Zachariah's health during the year deteriorated. He had been on
the verge of death several times in the past decade, and his strength
of will always brought him through. But the inevitable must prevail:
after a serious illness of many months, his seemingly unconquerable
spirit and determination were at last borne down. He died on 12 July
1755. Johnson wrote the following obituary for the newspapers:

On Saturday the 12th, about twelve at night, died Mr. Zachariah Williams, in his eighty-third year, after an illness of eight months, in full possession of his mental faculties. He has been long known to philosophers and seamen for his skill in magnetism, and his proposal to ascertain the longitude by a peculiar system of the variation of the compass. He was a man of industry indefatigable, of conversation inoffensive, patient of adversity and disease, eminently sober, temperate, and pious; and worthy to have ended life with better fortune.[22]

Johnson pasted this notice inside the cover of the twenty-one-page pamphlet he had written for Williams, and while at Oxford for a short visit late in the year, deposited the pamphlet in the Bodleian Library.[23]

Zachariah's death was a great loss, of course, to Miss Williams, but the urgency of her own condition muted her grief. She was yet in the utter depths of poverty. None of her literary efforts had succeeded. She survived only through Johnson's charity, and Johnson was not well-off himself. Nevertheless, he did nearly all in his power to find her an income, and now he hit upon a plan that turned out well. He prevailed upon his friend David Garrick, whose reputation as an actor was rapidly rising, to stage a benefit play in her behalf. Johnson himself tended to many of the details. He determined what kind of tickets would be needed, found a man who could design them, and recommended him for the necessary work to Edward Cave, the editor and publisher of the *Gentleman's Magazine*, who printed them. Writing to his acquaintances, Johnson urged them to buy tickets and begged them to urge *their* friends. The play chosen for the benefit was Aaron Hill's *Merope*. It was acted at Drury Lane Theatre on 22 January 1756 and brought Miss Williams £200, which being invested gave her a small but welcome return of interest.[24]

Francis returned from school at about this time. He was fourteen years old and more restless than ever. His absence from London had widened his experience of the world and had given him more self-confidence. He also possessed a great sense of independence, not having been required to follow orders or perform household chores in a long while. He hardly thought of himself as a servant, and he was legally no longer a slave; Colonel Richard Bathurst had recently died, and his will contained a clause giving Francis his freedom and the sum of twelve pounds.

At his return, Francis found Miss Williams firmly entrenched as a permanent occupant of the house and a tough character to get along with. She moved through the rooms, even down the treacherous stairs to the kitchen in the basement, with considerable ease and familiarity despite her blindness. She prepared her own meals— often little more than bread and butter—and frequently tended the tea pot. A visitor once remarked how easily she went about the house, searching into drawers and finding whatever she needed. "Believe me," said Miss Williams, "persons who cannot do these common offices without sight, did but little while they enjoyed that blessing."[25]

With her inherently dominant personality, and with Johnson occupied in the garret with his studies, Miss Williams naturally took command of running the household, telling Francis, whom she regarded as merely a black servant, what needed doing and scolding him when it was not done to her liking. She was strict and demanding, and Francis soon found life at Gough Square difficult to bear. Johnson was either unwilling or unable to lessen the tyranny that Miss Williams exercised over him. Perhaps Johnson did not fully realize the agony that Francis had to endure. Whatever the reason, the situation grew steadily worse until Francis could stand no more; being legally a freeman, and with several pounds in his pocket, he ran away.

He was taken in by a Mr. Farren, an apothecary in Cheapside, and began work as his assistant. Here he resided for nearly two years. During this time he often visited his former master in Gough Square, where Johnson received him with the same respect and kindness that he had always shown. Francis did not like being an apothecary's assistant, for the job was too menial and required too much work. Because of this, Johnson was able to persuade him to quit Mr. Farren and resume his old duties at Gough Square. It did not take long, however, for Francis to see that this would not do. Miss Williams seemed no less tyrannical than she had been two years earlier. Besides, at the age of sixteen, Francis yearned to get out and see something of the world. He dreamed of going to sea. Consequently, he was not back at Gough Square many weeks before he ran away again, this time heading for the coast.

He enlisted in the navy on 7 June 1758, aboard the Golden Fleece and was placed in the muster books as "L.M."—meaning "landsman"—a term applied to members of a ship's crew who are not trained seamen.[26] The Golden Fleece was the tender ship for HMS Princess Royal to which Francis was transferred at Sheerness three days later, on the 10th, and from her to HMS Stag on December 18th. The Stag was then under the command of Captain George Tindall, who was succeeded two months later, in February, by Captain Henry Angel.

Johnson sometimes spoke favorably of soldiering, but he held a violent and persistent hostility to seafaring. He said, "No man will be a sailor who has contrivance enough to get himself into a jail; for being in a ship is being in a jail, with the chance of being drowned."[27] He added, "A man in a jail has more room, better food, and commonly better company."[28] What he principally loathed about seafaring was the long confinement of a ship and the narrow compass of experience it affords the mind. Also, sailors were not known for their gentleness and God-fearing ways, and since Francis was not a hardy youngster, and since he was still at an impressionable age, Johnson not only feared for his safety, but also feared for his moral and spiritual well-being.

Wishing to get Francis out of the navy as soon as possible, Johnson spoke of his apprehensions to Tobias Smollett, the novelist. Smollett offered to write to his friend the notorious but influential John Wilkes. Johnson may have hesitated, for he detested Wilkes as a vile Whig and a character of low morals. Furthermore, Wilkes had once poked fun at an absurd statement Johnson made in his Dictionary, that "the letter H, seldom, perhaps never, begins any but the first syllable." Wilkes wrote in reply, "The author of this observation must be a man of quick *appre-hension*, and of a most *compre-hensive* genius."[29] Wilkes, however, knew several lords of the Admiralty, so that Johnson, in his concern for Francis, allowed Smollett to approach him. Smollett wrote to Wilkes as follows:

Chelsea, March 16, 1759

Dear Sir,

I am again your Petitioner in behalf of that great Cham of Literature, Samuel Johnson. His Black Servant, whose name is Francis Barber, has been pressed on board the

Stag Frigate, Capt. Angel, and our Lexicographer is in great Distress. He says the Boy is a sickly Lad of a delicate frame, and particularly subject to a malady in his Throat which renders him very unfit for his majesty's Service. You know what matter of animosity the said Johnson has against you, and I dare say you desire no other opportunity of resenting it than that of laying him under an obligation. He was humble enough to desire my assistance on this occasion, though he and I were never cater-cousins, and I gave him to understand that I would make application to my Friend Mr. Wilkes who perhaps by his Interest with Dr. Hay and Mr. Elliot might be able to procure the Discharge of his Lacquey. It would be superfluous to say more on the sub-ject which I leave to your Consideration, but I cannot let slip this opportunity of declaring that I am with the most inviolable Esteem and Attachment,

> Dear Sir,
>> your affectionate, obliged humble Servt.,
>> T:ˢ Smollett[30]

Wilkes applied to his friend, Dr. George Hay, one of the Lords Commissioners of the Admiralty, and on this request an order was made out for Francis's discharge. Unfortunately, Johnson was away from London at this crucial time when the final details required his presence. As a result, all of these efforts came to nothing, and Francis remained in the navy.

4 Robert Levett and No. 1 Inner Temple Lane

Now that the *Dictionary* was published, Johnson converted the garret of his Gough Square house into a study. It had been ideal as a workroom because it was large; yet being at the top of the house, up three flights of stairs, with its small windows admitting less light than the other rooms, it seemed an inconvenient place for a library. The spare bedroom, on the third floor, across from his own bedroom, would have been more commodious, but Johnson chose the garret because, as he told a friend, "in that room only I never saw Mrs. Johnson."[1] All other rooms in the house were simply too full of memories. The spare bedroom he put to use as a laboratory, where he experimented making elixir. When his friend Arthur Murphy first called at Gough Square, in the year 1754, to apologize for having translated into English and published an article taken from a French journal, only to discover that it was a recent *Rambler* essay, he found Johnson "all covered with soot like a chimney-sweeper, in a little room, with an intolerable heat and strange smell, as if he had been acting Lungs in the Alchymist."[2]

Into the garret Johnson moved his books. Most of them continued to lie in odd parts of the room where they were first set down, with no order being given their arrangement. Even rare Greek folios lay on the floor gathering dust. In one corner stood an old deal writing table littered with papers, and near it, propped against the wall, was a battered elbow chair missing an arm and a leg. With considerable dexterity Johnson would sit in this chair, balancing on its remaining three legs, and when he got up, he never forgot to return it to its position against the wall.[3]

Probably the spare bedroom, or laboratory, is where another

member of the Johnson household slept, though often, perhaps, he slept in the basement kitchen. This additional member was a part-time lodger named Robert Levett.[4] Johnson had known Levett since 1746. He had met him at Old Slaughter's Coffee House in St. Martin's Lane, much patronized by French émigrés. Johnson dropped into Slaughter's occasionally to improve his French. Levett was a poor and homeless man of middle age who earned a meager living as a "practitioner" of physic.

In England at this time there existed different levels of medical men.[5] Topmost came the physician. He was generally of good family, cultured, university educated, and if he practiced in London, was usually a fellow of the Royal College of Physicians. His chief value lay in his wide knowledge of diagnosis and the application of medicines.

Next came the surgeon. He was affiliated with a hospital. When a patient failed to respond to the physician's medicines, an operation was the next—and usually the last—resort. Anesthetics were as yet unknown so that for the patient surgery took a great deal of courage tempered with desperation, while the surgeon needed a quick, steady hand and usually three or four strong assistants. The surgeon was generally less educated and cultured than the physician, and mastery of his profession came through apprenticeship. The barber-surgeon was merely a surgeon not connected with a hospital, but who conducted a general practice.

The apothecary followed. In London, he was a licensed member of the Freemen of the Society of Apothecaries, and his job was to prepare and sell drugs. He was less educated and came from a lower class than either the surgeon or the physician, who were both highly respected men in society; but he was commonly the first line of defense against illness. Frequently, however, when faced with unusual or complex symptoms, he sought out the greater knowledge of the physician and paid him a fee for advice. Many physicians had practices in which all they did was advise apothecaries from a comfortable chair in the local tavern.

At the bottom of the scale came the unlicensed practitioner. He was not formally educated or trained in medicine, and he was not connected to a medical organization or officially recognized by any. His practice was among people too poor to afford the services of physicians or surgeons or even apothecaries. He was commonly a charitable and humane individual, poor himself, but dedicated to his profession. In this bottommost category of medical men was Robert Levett.

Levett (Johnson often spelled the name with only one *t*) was born in West Ella, in the parish of Kirk Ella, about five miles from Hull in Yorkshire, on 30 August 1705. He was the first of ten children born to Thomas Levit, farmer, and his wife, Elizabeth. He lived with his parents until he was nearly twenty and then moved to Hull where he became shopman to a woolen draper. Hungry for knowledge and already familiar with Latin, he was introduced by a neighbor of his employer to the practice of medicine. After two years with the woolen draper, he moved to London, hoping to learn more of medicine; but circumstances directed him elsewhere, and he became steward for a time to Lord Cardigan. Nevertheless, saving his money, he was soon able to visit France and Italy where he gained experience in the practice of physic. He later brought back with him into England a valuable medical library which he had collected on his travels, and he still had enough money left to apprentice one of his brothers to a mathematical instrument maker and to place another brother in school. Returning to France, he proceeded to Paris where he took a job as a waiter in a coffeehouse. Quickly he grew acquainted with the surgeons who came there. They were so pleased by his enthusiasm for medicine and his eagerness to learn from their conversation, that they took up a collection so that he could obtain decent instruction. They further got him free admission to lectures on anatomy and pharmacy delivered by some of the most learned men in their fields. After five years in Paris, Levett returned to London, took rooms in the house of an attorney in Northumberland Court near Charing Cross, and went forth into the city among the poorer classes of people as a practitioner of physic.

Johnson admired Levett for many reasons: he was dedicated to his work, commanded a wide-ranging though superficial knowledge of medicine (a subject that always fascinated Johnson), was hardworking, uncomplaining, charitable, and honest. Being destitute, he also enlisted Johnson's sympathy.

Levett's life had been a relatively hard one, and it showed in his features. Standing five-feet-five-inches tall, he looked considerably older than his fifty-four years. As a young man he had been thickset, dark complexioned, with a head of black hair; but he was now remarkably thin, gray haired, with a face cruelly scarred by small-pox. His manner was brusque, his carriage clumsy, and even Johnson confessed that his appearance and behavior were such that he disgusted the rich and terrified the poor. Some took his natural taciturnity as humble reserve while others saw in it a studied formality and haughtiness. The grotesque little man repulsed many of Johnson's friends, who could not understand why Johnson associated with him. But Johnson cared little for external appearances and perceived the unoffending selflessness of the man. Moved by admiration and his own deep sense of charity, Johnson provided Levett with a meal and a place to sleep whenever he needed it.

Johnson was not so poor as Levett, but by 1759 his income had dwindled to almost nothing. He had contracted with his publishers to receive for the *Dictionary* £1,575.[6] The money was paid to him by drafts over the seven years he was engaged on the work. The entire sum, plus an additional £200 due to an error in computation, had been paid off, and nearly all of it spent, by the time the *Dictionary* was published in April 1755. Once the cost of assistants, paper, books, and other needed materials was subtracted, Johnson's profit was rather small. Having, in consequence, to reduce his household expenses, Johnson reluctantly gave up his house in Gough Square. On 23 March 1759 he wrote his stepdaughter, Lucy Porter, in Lichfield:

Dear Madam

I beg your pardon for having so long omitted to write. One thing or other put me off. I have this day moved my things, and you are now to direct to me at Staple Inn London.[7]

Staple Inn is a group of buildings, erected in the 1580s, surrounding a cobblestone courtyard. The half-timbered front, with its many little shops, looks out on busy High Holborn. In Johnson's day, the place was considered unattractive, and the rent for a set of chambers ran about ten to twelve pounds a year. Johnson is thought to have taken the rooms upstairs, under the roof, at No. 2. The accommodations were small and cramped compared with the spacious house in Gough Square, so Miss Williams had to take a room of her own at a boarding school in Bolt Court, just around the corner from Gough Square.[8] She was not deprived of Johnson's company, however, for he made it a point to visit her over several cups of tea every evening before he retired for the night. As Johnson was a nocturnal creature, seldom getting to bed before two o'clock in the morning and sometimes later, his visits were commonly made after midnight. Miss Williams waited up, regardless of the hour, for this was the high point of her day—tea and intelligent conversation.

Johnson stayed only about eight months at his new lodgings in Staple Inn; by November he had moved into Gray's Inn, less than five minutes' walk from Staple Inn, just across Holborn and a little way up Gray's Inn Road.

Even with his own life so unsettled at this point, he continued to worry about Francis. Sixteen months had passed since Francis had joined the navy. His ship, the *Stag*, had been at Sheerness in May, at the Downs in early June, and was listed "at sea" in the latter part of June and during the months of October and November. To obtain Francis's release Johnson decided to apply directly to Wilkes's friend Dr. George Hay of the Admiralty. He explained the situation in a letter. He stated that Francis had run away to sea, that he wished to have him back, and that although an order for his discharge had been previously issued, he happened to be away from London at the time and so had received no advantage from it. He requested that Hay repeat the order "and inform me how to cooperate with it so that it may be made effectual."[9] (See Appendix B.)

The letter was slow in attaining its end, for the *Stag* put in at Leith Road early in December, where she remained for nearly two months with no action being taken in the matter. She put out to sea about the middle of February 1760, returning again to Leith Road by the end of the month. She then sailed to the Nore and to Sheerness in March; to the Nore again in April; "at sea" once more for most of April, May, and June; then into Torbay near the beginning of July. Finally, against his wishes, Francis was discharged by order of the Admiralty on 8 August 1760, seven months after Johnson's request. He had not, of course, been pressed into service as Smollett stated in his letter to Wilkes; he had gone voluntarily, and now he had no desire to return to land. He loitered about the ship for yet another two months while it was in port, and with much regret, he at last disembarked on the 22nd of October.[10]

When Francis returned to London he found Johnson residing at No. 1 Inner Temple Lane, about a quarter mile from the rooms he rented at Staple Inn. The new address was two doors down from the arch that led into the narrow lane from Fleet Street. Johnson had taken these slightly more spacious lodgings, for which he paid about fifteen or sixteen pounds annual rent, at the beginning of 1760 after only two months at Gray's Inn. He occupied rooms on the first floor. The apartments in this building were already considered old-fashioned. After ascending a few steps from the lane, one passed through the front door into "a dark and dingy old wainscotted anti-room" whose cold gloominess was only moderately dissipated by the light and warmth from the fireplace.[11] Johnson's books were kept at the top of the building, on the fourth floor, in two garrets which before were used as a bookseller's warehouse. Despite the dirt and dust that were usually a part of Johnson's dwellings, this library was bright and cheerful, for several large windows looked out over red brick roofs to St. Paul's Cathedral in the distance. In one of the garrets Johnson set up his chemical apparatus and often amused himself— and distressed his neighbors—by distilling substances from such things as peppermint and the dregs of strong beer, "from the latter whereof," said John Hawkins, "he was able to extract a strong but very noxious spirit which all might smell, but few chose to taste."[12]

Francis resumed his former duties—answering the door, running errands, and occasionally waiting table when company called. Even so, he found that he had considerable time on his hands and freedom enough to enjoy it. Without the hounding of Miss Williams, who still resided at the boarding school in Bolt Court, life was far more agreeable than it had been. He often kept company with friends of his own race—servants of other households in the neighborhood. One day the Reverend B. N. Turner called at Inner Temple Lane to see Johnson, but Johnson was not home, "and when Francis Barber, his black servant, opened the door to tell me so, a group of his African countrymen were sitting round a fire in the gloomy anti-room; and on their all turning their sooty faces at once to stare at me, they presented a curious spectacle."[13]

During the year 1760 and the one that preceded it, Johnson accomplished little; "he lived in poverty, total idleness, and the pride of literature."[14] He had, in April of 1758, begun writing a new series of articles called *The Idler*, which appeared every Saturday in *The Universal Chronical, or Weekly Gazette* and continued for two years, until April of 1760. These essays were generally less profound and polished

than the *Rambler* essays had been. Johnson often dashed them off
shortly before they were needed by the printer. The series was ap-
propriately titled, for *The Idler* reflected the general temper of Johnson's life at this time, while the articles themselves described the
miseries of idleness "with the lively sensations of one who has felt
them."[15]

Johnson was also engaged on a new edition of Shakespeare's
plays, but the work had progressed by only fits and starts for over a
decade. In 1745 he had published "Observations of Macbeth" as a
specimen of the projected edition. Eleven years later, in 1756, he
issued "Proposals for Printing, by Subscription, the Dramatick Works
of William Shakespeare, corrected and illustrated by Samuel Johnson," which promised that the work should be published "on or
before Christmas 1757."[16] In June of the promised year he assured
his friend Thomas Warton, "I am printing my new edition of Shak-
speare."[17] But to Charles Burney he had to confess that his Shakespeare would not be out so soon as he had expected: "It will,
however, be published before summer."[18] Yet the summer came and
went with no Shakespeare—and then another summer. In October
of 1762 the satiric poet, Charles Churchill, close friend of John Wilkes,
rebuked Johnson's procrastination:

> He for subscribers baits his hook,
> And takes their cash—but where's the book?
> No matter where—wise fear, we know,
> Forbids the robbing of a foe;
> But what, to serve our private ends,
> Forbids the cheating of our friends?[19]

If Johnson saw these lines they did little to bestir him. Nor
could he be moved by Sir Joshua Reynolds and other friends who
tried to engage him in a wager to complete the work by a specific
date. Johnson carried on with life at his usual pace.

His usual pace was slow and dilatory. He commonly arose early
in the afternoon, between noon and two o'clock, tarried over buns
and tea, and often frittered away the rest of the afternoon lost in
reverie, frequently tormenting himself with dismal thoughts of mor-
tality and sin. He went out usually about four o'clock for dinner to
a nearby tavern, often the Mitre Tavern in Fleet Street. There he
remained talking with acquaintances till late in the evening when

he made his nightly visit to Miss Williams before returning home. And so he filled up his day.

Arthur Murphy observed that Johnson's mind, strained and over-labored by constant exertion, had not yet regained its tone;[20] but other of Johnson's friends worried that the intellectual exertion of previous years had induced a serious and permanent mental decline. Alleyne Fitzherbert, Baron St. Helens, called at Johnson's one morning intending to send a letter from there into the city, but he was surprised to find "an author by profession without pen, ink, or paper."[21] Johnson himself grew concerned about his lethargy. On Easter Eve of 1761 he had reflected upon the year past and had written in his diary, "Since the Communion of last Easter I have led a life so dissipated and useless, and my terrours and perplexities have so much encreased, that I am under great depression and discouragement. . . ."[22]

Many of his afternoons were spent in conversation; his *Dictionary* had brought him a great reputation and with it many visitors: there were old friends and genuine well-wishers, would-be friends, and the idly curious, and also a few inevitable poltroons and sycophants. Johnson kindly received them all. His neighbor, who resided under the arch where Inner Temple Lane meets Fleet Street, said that more inquiries were made at his shop for Johnson "than for all the inhabitants put together of both the Inner and Middle Temple."[23]

Quite unexpectedly, in the midst of this idleness and poverty, good fortune suddenly befell him: King George III granted him a pension of £300 a year. Johnson was at first hesitant to accept this gift considering the definitions he had given the words *pension* and *pensioner* in his Dictionary:

> Pension. An allowance made to any one without an equiv-
>   alent. In England it is generally understood to
>   mean pay given to a hireling for treason to his
>   country.
> Pensioner. A slave of state hired by a stipend to obey his
>   master.

Furthermore, rumors quickly spread that his pension was a political bribe to appease Johnson's Jacobite sentiments and to induce him to become apologist of the present government. His friends assured him, however, that he need not hesitate accepting a reward from the

king for literary excellence; Sir Joshua Reynolds added that the definitions in his Dictionary certainly did not apply to him. And when
Johnson called on Prime Minister Lord Bute, to thank him for His
Majesty's generosity, Bute told him expressly, "It is not given you for
any thing you are to do, but for what you have done."[24]

The pension did little at first to alter Johnson's life. He continued to wear the same dirty clothes, and his lodgings retained the
same look of squalor. "Now that I have this pension," he said, "I am
the same man in every respect that I have ever been; I retain the
same principles." Smiling, he added,

> It is true, that I cannot now curse the House of Hanover;
> nor would it be decent for me to drink King James's health
> in the wine that King George gives me money to pay for.
> But, Sir, I think that the pleasure of cursing the House of
> Hanover, and drinking King James's health, are amply over-
> balanced by three hundred pounds a year.[25]

As for those who clamored that Johnson had been bought off, he
remarked, "I wish my pension were twice as large, that they might
make twice as much noise."[26]

More than anything, the pension allowed Johnson to exercise
greater beneficence toward the poor members of his household and
toward others close to him. This was demonstrated in an episode
concerning Levett. Early in 1762, Levett, who was now approaching
sixty, had become infatuated with a young woman whom he met
while visiting patients on his daily rounds of impoverished neigh-
borhoods. To impress her he said that he was a physician with a
large practice. She, in turn, told Levett that she was an heiress who
in time would be rich, the near relation of a man of wealth who
meanly contrived to keep her from her rightful possessions. Although
their place of rendezvous was a small coal shed in Fetter Lane, each
was convinced of the other's respectability and fortune. Only after a
hasty marriage did doubts begin to arise. In a letter to Joseph Baretti,
who was visiting his native Milan, Johnson wrote in July that "Levet
is lately married, not without suspicion that he has been wretchedly
cheated in his match."[27] The facade of mutual deception soon col-
lapsed and each saw the other as a fraud. Johnson then informed
Baretti of the truth: "Mr. Levet has married a street-walker."[28]

Less than four months following the wedding, a writ was issued against Levett for debts incurred by his wife. He went into hiding to avoid arrest, and Johnson managed to secure him the protection of a foreign minister. Shortly afterward, Levett's wife ran away and was soon taken into custody for picking pockets at the Old Bailey. Levett wanted to attend the trial, hoping she would be hanged, but Johnson, with much difficulty, prevented him. She pleaded her own cause and was acquitted. Johnson later said that compared with the marvels of this entire episode, the tales of the Arabian Nights Entertainment seemed like familiar occurrences.

Levett had stayed under Johnson's roof only occasionally before, but now Johnson took him in as a permanent member of the household. Besides simply providing shelter for a destitute creature, Johnson thought that a man nearly sixty years of age, who could persuade himself that a young woman of family and fortune was in love with him, required looking after.

The charity and beneficence that Johnson displayed after receiving his pension extended to others as well. He wrote to his stepdaughter, Lucy Porter, in Lichfield, saying, "If you are in any distress or difficulty, I will endeavour to make what I have, or what I can get, sufficient for us both."[29] To Miss Williams he gave an allowance and sought to bring some diversion into her tedious life by taking her with him on Sundays to dine with friends, where, "from her manner of eating, in consequence of her blindness, she could not but offend the delicacy of persons of nice sensations."[30] She sometimes accompanied him on longer jaunts to such places as Bishop's Stortford in Hertford and to Oxford. One day he asked David Garrick for a free ticket so that she might enjoy a play, yet for some reason Garrick declined. This lack of charity rankled Johnson, and with the incident smouldering in his mind, he dropped in late one Monday afternoon to the bookshop of Tom Davies in Russell Street.[31]

Davies was in the back room talking with a young Scottish acquaintance, but he saw Johnson through the glass door. Davies rushed out, brought Johnson back with him into the room, and made the necessary introductions: Mr. James Boswell—Mr. Samuel Johnson. The younger man, recalling rumors of Johnson's prejudice towards the Scots, said to Davies in mock distress, "Don't tell where I come from."

"From Scotland!" cried Davies.

"Mr. Johnson," said Boswell, with a strong burr, "I do indeed come from Scotland, but I cannot help it."

"That, Sir, I find," replied Johnson, "is what a very great many of your countrymen cannot help."

Boswell was momentarily stunned and embarrassed by this blunt reply to his pleasantry.

"What do you think of Garrick?" Johnson then asked Davies. "He has refused me an order [ticket] for the play for Miss Williams, because he knows the house will be full, and that an order would be worth three shillings."

"Oh, Sir," said Boswell, eager to gain upon Johnson's attention, "I cannot think Mr. Garrick would grudge such a trifle to you."

With a stern look, Johnson shot back, "Sir, I have known David Garrick longer than you have done: and I know no right you have to talk to me on the subject."

Mortified by this sharp rebuke, Boswell lapsed into silence. Had he been a proud man of delicate ego, this would have been the end of the relationship. He sat quietly for a time, however, listening to Johnson's rich and varied conversation. Later, when Davies excused himself to attend some business in the shop, Boswell ventured a few remarks that Johnson received courteously, and by the time Boswell rose to leave (for he had an engagement elsewhere), he was satisfied that while Johnson's manner was rough, he was not ill-natured.

A few days later, Boswell saw Davies again and asked if it would be proper for him to call on Johnson at his rooms in the Temple. Davies assured him that Johnson would take it as a compliment. Therefore, on Tuesday, May 24th, Boswell called at No. 1 Inner Temple Lane and was shown in. He noticed on entering that the rooms were filthy and the furniture battered and mismatched. Johnson himself was particularly slovenly: he wore a dirty brown coat and waistcoat along with brown trousers that had originally been crimson; his shirt neck was open, and the legs of his breeches were loose at the knees; and by way of slippers, he had on a pair of old unbuckled shoes.

Some weeks later, being taken up to the library by Levett, Boswell found these two garret rooms as filthy as the living quarters. Books lay all about in dust and confusion, and manuscript pages were strewn about the floor. In one room Boswell noted the alembic, retorts, receivers, and other apparatus for conducting simple chem-

ical experiments. Johnson told him that when he wanted to study
and not be interrupted, he secretly came up to the library without
telling Francis, for he would not allow Francis to say that he was out
when he was really at home: "If I accustom a servant to tell a lie for
me, have I not reason to apprehend that he will tell many lies for
himself?"[32]

The great untidiness of the apartments, so disconcerting to
visitors, even troubled Johnson from time to time. His notebook for
this period often echoes the sentiments he expressed on Good Friday, 1764: "I hope to put my rooms in order.... Disorder I have found
one great cause of Idleness."[33] But it was a hard resolution to keep.
He had never been good at keeping things clean or in order. His
wife had possessed "a particular reverence for cleanliness" that he
thought troublesome. She was fond of observing that a clean floor
was *so* comfortable, until Johnson one day exclaimed that they had
had enough talk about the floor and would now have a touch at the
ceiling.

His own personal cleanliness concerned him little. He thought
nothing of going into the country for a visit of several months and
not taking a change of clothing, and he declared openly that he had
no passion for clean linen.[34] Not many people in eighteenth century
England bathed, including Johnson. Only enthusiasts did so. Once
when a gentleman was propounding the healthful benefits of cold
baths, Johnson cut in with an inquiry after his health. When the man
assured him that it was good, Johnson said, "Then, Sir, let well
enough alone, and be content. I hate immersion."[35]

General standards of personal hygiene at this time were low
compared with those of today, or even compared with those of the
Middle Ages. Public baths had served the needs of Londoners up
until about the time of Elizabeth, but with the recurring outbreaks
of plague, like everything else of a public or communal nature, they
fell under suspicion of spreading infection.[36] Long after the horrors
of the plague had passed from living memory into history, when
people again crowded together at playhouses, carnivals, executions,
balls, and other places of public amusement, the notion persisted
that bathing was not altogether healthy, mainly because it lowered
resistance to infection. To the same degree that bathing was unpopular, merchants did a thriving business in perfumes, powders,
and pomatums with which to cover up less agreeable odors. Atti-

tudes toward personal cleanliness had begun changing in the eighteenth century, particularly in the later decades, but the change was slow, and those who inspired it were thought a trifle eccentric.

In 1734 Sir John Floyers published in the *Gentleman's Magazine* a "Treatise on Cold Baths." He claimed to have cured children of rickets by dipping them in a bath every morning, "and this wonderful Effect has encouraged me to dip four Boys at Litchfield [*sic*] in the Font of their Baptism, and none have suffer'd any Inconvenience by it."[37] Sir John apparently thought the beneficial effects of bathing were to be found in the coldness of the water, not in the amount of filth the water removed. So, too, did Dr. Charles Lucas who, in an article, made the extravagant statement that the old gentleman who takes cold baths will experience a return of uninterrupted health. "This instance does not prove that the cold bath produces health," insisted Johnson, who reviewed the article for the *Literary Magazine*, "but only, that it will not destroy it. He is well with the bath, he would have been well without it."[38]

Water was also hard to come by in eighteenth-century London, and this was another reason why bathing was unpopular and private baths unknown. Some of the newer London homes had water piped in from the Waterworks at London Bridge or from Merchants' Waterworks at the corner of St. Martin's Lane and Chandos Street. Other homes might get water from the New River or from Hampstead Ponds to the north. But the service was intermittent, water flowing through the pipes for only two or three hours three days a week. And the water passing through the spigot was none too pure. That coming from the Thames was perhaps the cleanest, and yet the Thames was polluted. Into it went the refuse of tanneries, slaughterhouses, vegetable markets, and uncounted thousands of chamber pots. Water closets, sewers, and methods of sewage treatment were as yet unknown. The Thames was both the main sewer system and the main source of water supply. Usually the contents of chamber pots were emptied into the kennel, the gutter running down the middle of the street; there the filth waited to be carried away by the next rain and washed into the river. Better appointed homes had closestools or cesspools which were more convenient, but they still had to be emptied periodically. If neglected, they casued trouble—as when Samuel Pepys, in the previous century, thought of putting in a window below stairs, "and going down into my cellar to look, I put my foot into a great heap of turds, by which I find that Mr. Turners house of office is full and comes into my cellar."[39] When properly tended these cesspools were emptied by "dustmen" and the contents piled onto local laystalls (dungheaps) near the river. When the mound grew high enough it was carted away in barges and sold to outlying farmers for fertilizer.

Even by the standards of the day, Johnson's personal habits—the filthy rooms, the dirty clothes, the unwashed hands—dismayed people entering his household and viewing his private life for the first time. Yet the dismay and repugnance were quickly swept aside by the power of his intellect and personality. Boswell was soon caught up in the force of the man's character and lost all sense of the dirty surroundings.

Johnson was likewise attracted to Boswell, whose easy, lively, disarming manner he found hard to resist. When the young man called again after an absence of two weeks, Johnson asked him why he did not come more often. Boswell replied that Johnson had not given him much encouragement and reminded him of the harsh treatment he had received at their first meeting in Davies' bookshop. "Poh, poh! never mind these things. Come to me as often as you can. I shall be glad to see you."[40]

The next time Boswell met Johnson it was in the company of Oliver Goldsmith at the Mitre Tavern. Boswell had known Goldsmith for some time, and before Johnson arrived, Boswell, in the course of conversation, mentioned Levett, whom he thought "a curious-looking little man."[41] "He is poor and honest," said Goldsmith, "which is recommendation enough to Johnson." Yet Boswell wondered why Johnson was so kind to a man who was rumored to be so haughty and unpleasant. "He is now become miserable," answered Goldsmith, "and that ensures the protection of Johnson."[42]

Following the evening's conversation, as the hour grew late and the gathering began to break up, Johnson rose to make his usual call on Miss Williams for tea. Accompanying Johnson on one of these nightly visits to Bolt Court was considered a great privilege. Boswell, therefore, envied Goldsmith, who, as he strutted away with Johnson into the night, called over his shoulder with an air of superiority, "I go to Miss Williams." It was not long, however, before Boswell became a privileged man himself when Johnson took him to visit Miss Williams one afternoon for tea. "I found her a facetious, agreeable woman, though stone-blind," he recorded in his journal.[43] What he particularly liked about Miss Williams was her conversation, for she was knowledgeable in literature, and she expressed herself well. Furthermore, through her eleven year association with Johnson, she was well acquainted with his habits and knew how to lead him on to talk. This was, at times, of great value, for Johnson often sat in company for long periods of time without saying a word. Tom Tyers told him one day that he was like a ghost: he never spoke till he was spoken to.[44]

It was not long after this that Boswell left England for Utrecht, Holland, where he was to undertake the study of law. Johnson went with him to Harwich to see him aboard his ship. After this brief journey, Johnson returned to the Temple, where he resumed a life more indolent than ever. His pension gave him enough financial independence that he did not need to write for a living, and therefore he did little of it.

For what he had already written he received in 1765 a second honorary degree: he was made Doctor of Laws by Trinity College, Dublin. He acknowledged his gratitude in a letter to Dr. Thomas Leland, though privately he valued more the degree of M.A. from his own university, Oxford. But far more important than this degree was the acquaintance he made early in the year with Henry Thrale and his twenty-four-year-old wife, Hester.

Thrale was a wealthy brewer of Southwark, educated at Oxford, and thirty-six years of age. He was tall, well-proportioned, intelligent, even-tempered, and something of a beau. Arthur Murphy, who knew both Johnson and Thrale, spoke so glowingly of Johnson's moral and literary character that Thrale was anxious to meet him. Mrs. Thrale was even more eager, having heard Johnson's powers of conversation praised many years before by William Hogarth, for whom she claimed to have sat for the preliminary sketches for *The Lady's Last Stake*.[45] As a pretext to lure Johnson to their home, the Thrales invited the "shoemaker poet," James Woodhouse, to dine, then invited Johnson to meet him. They were only mildly impressed by Woodhouse, but they took to Johnson immediately; in fact, they were so much pleased by this great and ungainly man, and he so gratified with their attentions to him, that every Thursday evening for the rest of the winter, Johnson drove out to Southwark for dinner. In a short time he would speak of the Thrale residence as "home," finding in it the comfort and peace soon denied him in his own household.

5   "Good of myself I know not
where to find, except a little
Charity."

In October of 1765 appeared at last *The Plays of William Shakespeare, in Eight Volumes, with the Corrections and Illustrations of Various Com-
mentators; To which are added Notes by Sam. Johnson.* The work would never
rank among Johnson's greatest productions (except for the preface,
which Adam Smith called "the most *manly* piece of criticism that
was ever published in any country"), but the public thought well
enough of it that it went through several editions.[1]

Johnson now found himself with enough money from his *Shakespeare* and from his pension to move back into a house; so in September of 1765 he left his rooms in the Temple and took up residence
at No. 7 Johnson's Court, Fleet Street. This narrow court was named
for one Thomas Johnson, a merchant tailor in the time of Queen
Elizabeth.[2] Johnson quickly brought Miss Williams into the house,
where she took a room on the first floor. Levett occupied the garret,
and Francis slept in the basement. One of the upper rooms, which
was airy and admitted plenty of light, Johnson began fitting up as a
study. On 7 March 1766, he made a notation in his diary under the
heading "ENTRING N. M. |NOVUM MUSEUM|":

> Almighty and most merciful Father, who hast graciously
> supplied me with new conveniences for study, grant that I
> may use thy gifts to thy glory.[3]

"New conveniences for study" referred to the many books he had
recently bought and begun setting up in cases, to the handsome
new furniture that now adorned the room, and to the prints hanging
on the walls. "I wish you were in my new study," he wrote to his

51

friend Bennet Langton, "I am now writing the first letter in it. I think it looks very pretty about me."[4]

The rest of the house he began furnishing also, and he went to the expense of purchasing a silver standish, silver salvers, and good plates for entertaining guests. John Hawkins observed that he successfully banished the appearance of squalid indigence which formerly disgusted those who came to see him. Yet, while the *appearance* of Johnson's household changed noticeably, the daily routine within it remained much the same. Whoever called at Johnson's Court about midday usually found Johnson and Levett sitting over a breakfast of butter and rolls, both silent, Levett pouring out tea, Johnson disheveled as having just risen from bed. In the evenings he was often invited out to dinner. But no matter how late he returned home, he never missed taking late night tea with Miss Williams—or rather Mrs. Williams as she was being called, having passed her sixtieth birthday.

Being in greater daily contact with Johnson, living as she did once again under his roof, Mrs. Williams began inquiring about her book that had been so long neglected. Fifteen years had passed since the "Proposals" for her "Essays in Prose and Verse" appeared in the *Gentleman's Magazine*, and during that time nothing much had been done. She had depended on Johnson to aid her in the venture, but over the years he had been either too busy or too idle to do anything. She complained to a friend that whenever she brought up the subject "the Doctor always puts me off with 'Well, we'll think about it.'"[5] Goldsmith told her to leave everything to him, but he was temperamentally incapable of helping her publish a book, nor could he move Johnson to action.

The book had originally been offered for sale by subscription at five shillings, half to be paid on subscribing and the rest on delivery of the volume, unbound, in blue paper covers. The money she got from this canvassing was to have been used for publishing expenses; however, it had long ago been spent on personal necessities, and she agonized over appearing to have defrauded her subscribers. She finally gave up on Johnson and turned to several other friends for help. Elizabeth Carter, poet and writer, whom Johnson highly respected as a woman who could make a delicious pudding as well as translate Epictetus, supplied Mrs. Williams with a long list of names. Two other friends got in touch with these people, raising a new subscription at the full price of the volume, and in a short time collected sixty pounds. With most of the tedious drudgery of subscription selling over, and matters only of literary consequence remaining, Johnson took renewed interest in the project. When he perceived that Mrs. Williams's writings alone would make but a very slim volume, he offered to contribute some pieces of his own. He also got Mrs. Thrale to put down on paper a tale she had heard about Death coming to old Farmer Dobson; she turned it into verse and called it "The Three Warnings." Johnson supplied Mrs. Williams with "Epitaph on Philips," "Friendship, an Ode," a paraphrase from the Proverbs called "The Ant," and a fairy tale entitled "The Fountains." He also helped revise several of Mrs. Williams's own pieces, especially "On the Death of Stephen Gray, the Electrician."

Tom Davies published the book, 184 pages in large type, in April under the title *Miscellanies in Prose and Verse*. Its success was not great, however. Mrs. Thrale later wrote that the book "turned out a thin flat quarto, which it appears sold miserably: I never saw it on any table but my own."[6] The small income that it produced was put out at interest in the same way as the money received from the benefit play ten years earlier.

Johnson's failure all those years to assist Mrs. Williams with her book, and the neglect of his own work, was indicative of his uncertain emotional condition. He suffered throughout most of his life from melancholia, a neurosis characterized by extreme depression and bodily complaints. Although it fluctuated in its severity, he was never totally free of its torments, and at least twice in his life it brought him very near to a complete emotional breakdown. One of those times occurred in the spring of 1766 when his mental condition grew so depressed that, according to Mrs. Thrale, "he could not stir out of his room in the court he inhabited for many *weeks* together, I think months."[7] Johnson had already confided to the Thrales "the horrible condition of his mind, which he said was nearly distracted," but he swore them to "odd solemn promises of secrecy on so strange a subject."[8] One day Dr. William Adams, an old friend, paid Johnson a visit and found him in "a deplorable state, sighing, groaning, talking to himself, and restlessly walking from room to room." At last Johnson said to him, "I would consent to have a limb amputated to recover my spirits."[9]

The Thrales, although aware of Johnson's affliction, did not fully realize its seriousness until one day they called on him at his house where they found him in the company of Dr. John Delap, rector of Ilford and Kingston, a shallow sort of man who prided himself on being a poet and a dramatist. Johnson was on his knees before Delap when the Thrales entered, begging Delap for his prayers and "beseeching God to continue to him the use of his understanding."[10] Embarrassed at being discovered in so delicate a situation, Delap disengaged himself from Johnson to leave, but Johnson called after him in such a shocking manner of self-deprecation that Henry Thrale "involuntarily lifted up one hand to shut his mouth."[11] Realizing then how grave was Johnson's illness, the Thrales prevailed upon him to quit his house and to live with them for a time at Streatham Park, their country home. At Streatham Johnson could be cared for properly and brought back to health.

Streatham Park lay about six miles from the city on what is now Tooting Bec Road. The main residence, a three-story rectangular brick house, stood in a park of a hundred acres, which also contained farm buildings, stables, and greenhouses. Later, the main house was remodeled to include a large parlor and a library, and the grounds were improved by the addition of an extensive lawn, a summer house, and a lake with a small island in the middle.[12]

Johnson remained here for more than three months, from the middle of June till the first of October 1766. Francis often came out to Streatham, but when London promised greater entertainment, Johnson allowed him to return home.

Tranquillity seemed to permeate life at Streatham. Soon the comforts of a wealthy household, the spacious grounds to roam about in, and the solicitude of the Thrales wrought a healthy change in Johnson's spirits. He was surrounded by congenial society when he wished to be, got sufficient exercise, and ate the best food. A leg of pork boiled till it fell from the bone, veal pie with raisins and sugar, or the outside cut of a salt buttock of beef were his favorite dishes. Fresh fruit he considered a great delicacy, and in the kitchen garden grew peaches, melons, grapes, and nectarines. He usually ate seven or eight large peaches before breakfast and a like quantity after dinner.

Not only Johnson's physical and emotional health improved under these conditions, but Henry Thrale saw to it that his outward appearance also changed for the better. Streatham was no place for

Johnson's customary shabby, dirty clothes, frazzled wig, and unwashed hands. Thrale insisted that Johnson's clothes be cleaned,
that he change his shirt more often, and that silver buckles be put
on his shoes.

Johnson's eyes were so bad that at night he read with the candle
and book up close to his face. Mrs. Thrale said that when he read in
bed, as was his custom, it was a perpetual miracle he did not set
himself on fire. Still, for this reason, his wigs were in a sorry state;
the foretops of them all were singed down to the network. To ensure
that Johnson was presentable to company in the evening, Thrale
stationed a servant at the parlor entrance to hand Johnson a new
wig when he came down for dinner and to take it back again when
Johnson went back upstairs to his room.

Not long after returning to his own household, Johnson began
planning an extended visit to Lichfield for the upcoming months of
summer, and he thought this an appropriate time to place Francis
back in school. Therefore, in April of 1767, Francis resumed his education under the Reverend Joseph Clapp, headmaster of the grammar school in Bishop's Stortford, some thirty miles from London on
the road toward Cambridge. Francis boarded with Headmaster Clapp,
but then, in November, Clapp suddenly died, and Francis thought
that he might be called back to London. Johnson, however, wrote to
him saying, "I would have you stay at Mrs. Clapp's for the present,
till I can determine what we shall do. Be a good boy. My compliments
to Mrs. Clapp and to Mr. Fowler."[13]

The Mr. Fowler to whom Johnson sent his compliments was the
Reverend Robert Fowler, lately of St. Mary Magdalene College, Cambridge, elected by the school trustees to take Mr. Clapp's place. Fowler, however, did not like his position, and in January of the following
year, the trustees elected the Reverend William Ellis, M.A., to suc-
ceed him. This was about the time that the school moved from its
badly decayed building in High Street (where it had been since 1721)
to Mrs. Clapp's Tudor home, Windhill House, "till a new school shall
be built on another place provided by the Trustees."[14]

Francis was now twenty-two years of age and older than most
of his comrades. He was a competent though not exceptional stu-
dent; he could read and write English tolerably well, was advancing
slowly in Latin and Greek, but held out little hope of becoming a
scholar. Nevertheless, Johnson wrote to him, "I am very well satisfied

with your progress, if you can really perform the exercises which you are set. . . . Let me know what English books you read for entertainment. You can never be wise unless you love reading." He closed by saying, "Do not imagine that I shall forget or forsake you; for if, when I examine you, I find that you have not lost your time, you shall want no encouragement, from Yours affectionately, Sam: Johnson."[15]

Although Johnson was more financially secure during this period of his life than he had been previously, Mrs. Williams remained as poor as ever. The interest obtained from her invested capital was still insufficient to maintain her, and she hated being dependent upon Johnson's charity, particularly on the allowance he gave her. To help ease her mind and his own purse, Johnson thought it a good idea to try staging another benefit play, the first having been so successful in raising money thirteen years earlier. He considered it useless to approach David Garrick again, for Garrick seemed too preoccupied these days with his own successful career as actor and manager of Drury Lane Theatre to interest himself in personal charities. He therefore went to George Colman the dramatist, and manager of Covent Garden Theatre. Colman had been a friend and associate of Garrick for many years, but in purchasing Covent Garden Theatre, he had set himself up as a rival producer and so earned Garrick's animosity.

Colman agreed to stage the benefit play, and Johnson, in a letter to him, requested that he choose the play to be acted and appoint a day which could first be spared to perform it. Yet before the details could be worked out, William Powell, Colman's longtime friend, partner, and principal actor, suddenly died. The loss to Colman was great, both personally and professionally, and in the confusion and distress that followed, the plans for Mrs. Williams's benefit were laid aside and never taken up again.

Meanwhile, Boswell had returned from two years of study and travel on the continent and was practicing law in Scotland. He preferred the life of London to that of Edinburgh, and he made the long journey south whenever he could get away. Once in London, he contrived to be in Johnson's company as often as possible. He reveled in the pleasure of being intimate with so great a man. He was, at first, highly elated in just being allowed to partake in the daily ceremony of late night tea drinking with Mrs. Williams. "I willingly drank cup after cup, as if it had been the Heliconian spring," he recorded in his journal.[16] But the charm and novelty of the ritual soon wore off, mainly because Mrs. Williams brewed the tea herself, and when she poured it out, she determined when the cups were full by putting her finger down inside a little way until she felt the tea touch it.

Other of Johnson's friends were disgusted by Mrs. Williams's table manners, especially her feeding herself with her fingers. Baretti, for one, dined with Johnson as seldom as possible, for "I hated to see the victuals paw'd by poor Mrs. Williams, that would often carve, though stone blind."[17]

Johnson was not so fastidious. He freely relinquished to her the duties of the kitchen; in fact, he let her run the entire household. He did so not only because it helped her fill up an otherwise tedious and empty existence, but also because he was temperamentally unfitted for the daily cares of running it himself. Yet given the domestic power she wielded, together with the frustrations attendant upon her blindness and the circumscribed life it forced upon her, she grew increasingly overbearing and peevish in her disposition. Johnson unwittingly encouraged this, for he indulged her outbursts of ill temper, thinking it unchristian and uncharitable to check such a poor, miserable creature as she. Johnson, in fact, rather stood in awe of Mrs. Williams and her temper.

Despite her occasional peevishness, the good qualities for which she was known—her intelligence, piety, animated conversation, strong will, and commonsense—continued undiminished. She remained meticulous in her carriage and dress, appearing in company typically clothed in the French fashion, sometimes dressed in scarlet, her grey hair protruding from under a lace cap, a black lace hood over it, with two stiffened wings projecting out from the temples.

Although she was an object of charity herself, Mrs. Williams strove to be charitable to others in turn. She belonged to a group of women that helped support and manage The Ladies' Charity School, a Christian organization founded in King Street, Snow Hill, in 1702. Its original purpose was to give clothing to poor girls and, at the same time, to instruct them "in Christian principles and a sense of moral duty."[18] The results fell short of expectations, however, because the parents of these girls set poor examples of Christian principles and moral duty themselves, and also because they allowed their daughters to play in the streets, "where they seldom failed of hearing all manner of profane discourse."[19] To help remedy this, the women trustees of the school decided in 1755 that some of these girls should be boarded at the schoolhouse. Their parents and relations could visit them on Thursday afternoons, but at no other times.

The girls who were thus admitted, all of them between the ages of eight and ten, learned not only their prayers and catechism, but they were also taught reading, writing, sewing, and knitting. At the age of twelve they learned how to perform household work such as cleaning, washing, and ironing, and at fourteen they were bound out for five years as apprentices to creditable families. This training and apprenticeship, it was hoped, would eventually turn these previously destitute children into "useful and sober servants, and lead them to eternal happiness."[20]

Mrs. Williams often attended the meetings at the schoolhouse, held on the second Wednesday of every month between the hours of four and seven, where the female subscribers conducted the school's business. She saw to it that Johnson became a subscriber, and she was instrumental in later getting Mrs. Thrale to join the women trustees. Mrs. Williams was so zealous a supporter of the school that she made it the sole beneficiary in her will.

Johnson, by this time, had recovered his emotional stability. The first two years of the 1770s were among the serenest of his life. The other members of the household carried on with their own affairs with little disturbance or interruption. While Johnson spent a great deal of time with the Thrales at Streatham, Levett worked hard among the families too poor to find other medical help. Francis continued his studies in Bishop's Stortford, and Mrs. Williams visited longtime friends of her own, particularly the Wilkinson sisters. In one of Mrs. Williams's few extant letters (in the hand of an amanuensis, but signed by Mrs. Williams), we gain some feeling for the uneventful tenor of life in Johnson's household during this period. The letter is to Mrs. Percy, wife of Dr. Thomas Percy, who edited *Reliques of Ancient English Poetry*:

Madam,

Having been out of Town about three Weeks, I had the pleasure at my return to hear of Dear Mrs. Piercey's being safely delivered of a Daughter. Pray God give you joy of her.

I am anxious to know how yourself, Doctor Piercey & your little Family do. Doctor Johnson is constantly at Stratham, but whenever he comes to Town asks me, if I know how Mrs. Piercey does. Therefore, dear Madam that I may be satisfied myself & able to answer the Doctor's Question, let my dearest Favourite Miss Bab take up her Pen & write me a Letter of the fullest Information. I have no material News to send you, but that all our Neighbours are well & Doctor Johnson & myself have kept our healths tolerably all the Summer. My most respectful Compliments to Doctor Piercey, yourself & little Family. My sincerest wishes for your health I remain

Madam,
Your most obedient & most
humble Servant
Anna Williams[21]

August 5th 1772

Francis returned from school in 1772 and took up his former duties of answering the door, running errands, and buying provisions. He had not progressed in school as far as Johnson hoped he would. For one thing, he was at an age when youthful frolics took precedence over studies, and young women were of greater interest to him than Latin or Greek. His good-natured personality and pleasant features made him attractive to women, and Johnson occasionally found it necessary to put restraints upon his lovemaking. Mrs. Thrale one day confessed to Johnson that Francis was quite good looking "for a Black a moor." "Madam," Johnson replied, "Francis has carried the empire of Cupid farther than many men," and he told her that while away at school, Francis "made hay" with so much dexterity "that a female haymaker followed him to London for love."[22]

With Francis back home, the tranquillity of Johnson's household began deteriorating. Soon the old antagonisms between Francis and Mrs. Williams again flared into open hostilities. Mrs. Williams found Francis too independent, too neglectful of his chores, and too inattentive to his master's interests. Francis, on the other hand, chafed under the severe authority that Mrs. Williams attempted to exercise over him. Each of them complained to Johnson about the other, though Mrs. Williams was more insistent and peremptory in her accusations. She reproached Johnson for having squandered so much money (about £300) in a foolish attempt to have a thankless, lazy servant taught Latin and Greek. She would exclaim, "Here is your scholar! your philosopher! upon whom you have spent so many hundred pounds!"[23]

In the spring of 1773, Boswell came down to London, and Johnson invited him for dinner Easter day. He was surprised at receiving such an invitation, for he had never heard of Johnson entertaining dinner guests and assumed that he never did; Johnson seemed always to take his dinners in a tavern. Consequently, he was anxious to find out what a dinner at Johnson's house would be like. He did not know the influence the splendid meals at the Thrales were working upon Johnson's own table. "I supposed we should scarcely have knives and forks, and only some strange, uncouth, ill-drest dish."[24] Instead, he found a good dinner of soup, boiled leg of lamb, spinach, a veal pie, and rice pudding. The only other company were Mrs. Williams and a Miss Carmichael.

Miss Carmichael was a young Scottish woman; she may have been the prostitute that Johnson found lying in the street one night, too tired and weak to move. Johnson lifted her up onto his back and carried her to his house. There he had her cared for while she regained her health and strength. He discovered in talking with her that poverty had led her into prostitution.

Miss Carmichael claimed to be heir to a small patrimony that was now due her, but from which she was being excluded. Johnson told her that he would look into the matter, and at the first opportunity he discussed the subject with Robert Chambers, Vinerian Professor of Laws at Oxford University and soon to be appointed judge of the supreme court of judicature in Bengal, India. Chambers advised Johnson to get an attorney, for Miss Carmichael's only recourse was through the courts, and such maneuvering required specialized legal training. Unfortunately, neither Miss Carmichael nor Johnson could afford the services of an attorney, and so Johnson had to find one willing to take on the job gratis. He therefore wrote to Sir John Hawkins, asking for help. "I know few attorneys," he said, "and none so well as Mr Clark, yet I cannot venture to ask him to do business for nothing, but should think it a great favour if you would recommend the cause to him."[25]

Richard Clark was now thirty-three years old, but Johnson had known him since he was fifteen. The two had been introduced to each other by Hawkins. Clark liked mixing in literary society, often making one of the group to dine in Johnson's company at the Mitre Tavern, so it was predictable that when Hawkins approached him, Clark was happy to assist Johnson in any way he could. Johnson followed this up with a letter to him in February:

> Sir John Hawkins told me that you would be so kind as to undertake the business which I recommended to him and you. Mr. Chambers is now in town, and will be glad to consider the manner of proceeding with you.[26]

While these tedious legal proceedings were getting under way in London, up north Boswell was making final preparations for an excursion with Johnson through the Highlands of Scotland. He had been trying to get his friend into Scotland for years and many times felt close to succeeding, but he had been so often disappointed that he nearly despaired of ever achieving his goal; yet in the spring of 1773, Johnson at last resolved to make the trip. With Robert Chambers accompanying him part of the way, he arrived in Edinburgh the 14th of August, shortly after the Court of Session had risen. Francis was to have come along, but Boswell had already arranged to take with them his own man, Joseph Ritter, "a Bohemian, a fine stately fellow above six feet high."[27] In order to keep down expenses, Francis remained behind.

During the next three months, Boswell and Johnson traveled up the eastern coast of the Highlands to St. Andrews, Aberdeen, Inverness, and down to Fort Augustus; then to the Hebrides where they visited the isles of Skye, Rassay, Coll, Mull, Inchkenneth, and Icolmkill, returning to Edinburgh by way of Inveraray, along Loch Lomond to Dumbarton, then to Glasgow, Auchinleck (Boswell's family seat), and Hamilton.

Johnson was back in London by the end of November, but now he had a taste for travel, and in July of the following year, he set out with Henry and Hester Thrale for a two-month journey into Wales.

It was also in 1774 that the Reverend William Hetherington, "probably the richest clergyman in England,"[28] transferred to the governors of Christ's Hospital £20,000 in South Sea Annuities, and with this money established a charity for blind persons. The charity offered an annual stipend of £10 to qualified persons who were selected. In October, Mrs. Williams filled out a "paper of Enquiries" establishing her eligibility, and the paper was delivered to the counting house of Christ's Hospital. Five days later, application forms were handed out to all petitioners. Johnson wrote to John Perkins, the reliable, levelheaded superintendent of Thrale's brewery, asking him to stop by the hospital and pick up one of the petitions. "I àm a bad manager of business in a Croud," he explained, "and if I should send a mean Man, he may be sent away without his errand."[29] Francis delivered the letter to Perkins with instructions to go with him to the hospital and to bring home the petition once Perkins had it. The form was filled out and delivered back to the hospital. After a brief period of waiting, Mrs. Williams learned that her petition had been unsuccessful. She did not know at the time that it had little chance from the start, for over seven hundred people had applied for only fifty vacancies.

In the spring of the following year, 1775, Johnson received the highest honor Oxford University could bestow on him—an honorary diploma of Doctor of Laws. Boswell was in London at the time and was often in the company of his friend. They sometimes chatted in the evenings, then "he and I drank tea with Mrs. Williams in the old style."[30] Boswell noted that Johnson was highly pleased with his degree but did not vaunt his new dignity.

Boswell, this year, also had the honor of once again sitting to Easter dinner under Johnson's roof. This time he feasted heartily on soup, beef à la mode, boiled pork with pease pudding and potatoes, roast lamb, spinach, porter and port.

Mrs. Williams was now almost seventy, and her health began declining. Johnson grew concerned. In a postscript to a letter written to Mrs. Thrale on the day he received his Doctor of Laws degree, he informed her that "poor Mrs. Williams is very bad, worse than I ever saw her."[31] His letters during the ensuing months reported no improvement. "Mrs. Williams's pimples continue to come out and go in."[32] Wishing to cheer her up, Johnson suggested to Mrs. Thrale that "it would do her good, if you would send a message of enquiry, and a few strawberries or currants."[33] Mrs. Thrale later informed Johnson that she had sent "a pretty Pine Apple & a Bunch of Hothouse Grapes, & will call on her when I go to Town some Day."[34] Johnson was out of town when Mrs. Thrale paid her call, but he learned from Mrs. Williams "that you had honoured her with a visit and *behaved lovely*."[35]

Mrs. Montagu, one of the noted Blue Stockings of the period, was a friend of Mrs. Thrale, and it was probably from her that she learned of Mrs. Williams's poor health. Mrs. Montagu may never have met Mrs. Williams, but she knew of her reputation as a pious woman of superior abilities who suffered the misfortune of being poor and blind. Motivated by nothing more than charitable goodwill, she sent Mrs. Williams an envelope containing a draft for ten pounds and a letter informing her that she could expect the same grant every year. Mrs. Williams, surprised and elated, wrote to thank Mrs. Montagu the same day:

> Johnson's Court, 26th June, 1775
>
> Madam,—Often have I heard of generosity, benevolence, and compassion, but never have I known or experienced the reality of those virtues, till this joyful morning, when I received the honour of your most tender and affectionate letter with its most welcome contents. Madam, I may with truth say, I have not words to express my gratitude as I ought to a lady, whose bounty has, by an act of benevolence, doubled my income, and whose tender, compassionate assurance has removed the future anxiety of trusting to chance, the terror of which only could have prompted me to stand a publick candidate for Mr. Hetherington's bounty. May my sincere and grateful thanks be accepted by you, and may the Author of all good bless and long continue a life, whose shining virtues are so conspicuous and exemplary, is the most ardent prayer of her who is, with greatest respect, Madam, your most devoted, truly obliged, and obedient humble servant,
>
> Anna Williams[36]

Mrs. Montagu's gift was actually closer to a third than to half of Mrs. Williams's income, for at about this time, Lady Philips, wife of Sir John Philips, the man who had befriended Zachariah Williams by getting him admitted to the Charterhouse, together with some other Welsh ladies, began contributing a small amount toward Mrs. Williams's maintenance. Her income stood now at about thirty-five to forty pounds a year. Later, Miss Jane Wilkinson, one of the sisters who had helped her with her first book, left Mrs. Williams some money in a will, but the will was so poorly executed that Mrs. Williams most likely saw none of it.

In March of 1776, Johnson moved from his house in Johnson's Court to a larger, three-story brick house in Bolt Court. This narrow, freestone paved court is where Mrs. Williams had occupied rooms in a boarding school when Johnson moved to Staple Inn years before. Johnson rented the house, No. 8, at forty pounds a year from Edmund Allen, the printer, who lived in the house next door. Mrs. Williams occupied one of the rooms on the ground floor, and Johnson moved his books into the rooms on the floor above, making one of them his study. A small plot of ground in back of the house he planned to turn into a garden.

Less than a month after settling in at Bolt Court, he considered moving again. He liked his new house well enough, and he thought this particular area around Fleet Street the best situation in all of London, but he saw the opportunity of saving his forty pounds yearly rent when he learned that some of the apartments at Hampton Court, several miles up river, were coming vacant. The use of these apartments was granted to those of His Majesty's subjects who had performed distinguished service to their country. Johnson wrote to the Lord Chamberlain asking for one of these lodgings:

> Such a grant [he said] would be considered by me as a great favour; and I hope that to a man who has had the honour of vindicating his Majesty's government, a retreat in one of his houses may not be improperly or unworthily allowed. I therefore request that your lordship will be pleased to grant such rooms in Hampton Court as shall seem proper to
>
> My Lord,
> Your Lordship's most obedt. and
> most faithful humble servant
> Sam. Johnson[37]

The Lord Chamberlain replied that he was sorry he could not obey Johnson's commands, "having already on his hands many engagements unsatisfied."[38]

By the middle of summer, Mrs. Williams was still no better, and the household was further alarmed when Levett, now seventy-one years old, fell down and seriously hurt himself. Within a few months, however, he was mended and in perfect health, routinely walking five or ten miles every day on his rounds visiting patients. Still, Mrs. Williams remained the same. Levett prescribed for her as did Johnson's good friend, Dr. Thomas Lawrence, president of London's College of Physicians, but nothing seemed to have much effect. Johnson informed Boswell that

> Mrs. Williams, whom you may reckon as one of your well-wishers, is in a feeble and languishing state, with little hope of growing better. She went for some part of the autumn into the country, but is little benefited; and Dr. Lawrence confesses that his art is at an end. Death is, however, at a distance; and what more than that can we say of ourselves? I am sorry for her pain, and more sorry for her decay. Mr. Levett is sound, wind and limb.[39]

A month later, he again informed Boswell that Mrs. Williams had been very ill, "and though she is something better, is likely, in her physician's opinion, to endure her malady for life, though she may, perhaps, die of some other."[40]

This year, as Mrs. Williams declined and Robert Levett grew better, Francis Barber got married. He wed a twenty-year-old white woman named Elizabeth, whom Johnson immediately began calling Betsy. Betsy was charming and pretty, and although several disapproving eyebrows were raised over this interracial marriage, Johnson looked upon the match with equanimity and welcomed Betsy into the household.

Johnson's birthday was the 18th of September and Queeney's, the Thrales' eldest daughter, was the 17th. Every year, to celebrate both birthdays, the Thrales put on a dance and supper for their servants and their servants' friends, putting the summer house at their disposal during these two days "to fill with acquaintance and merriment."[41] Francis, of course, was always invited, and this year he and his wife were the center of attention. Johnson, writing to Levett in Bolt Court to say that he was soon going with the Thrales to Brighton for a brief stay, remarked with some pride that "Francis and his Wife have both given great satisfaction by their behaviour."[42]

Johnson's health, while never excellent, had at least been fairly stable during the past several years, but in January of 1777 he began experiencing great difficulty in breathing, particularly when he lay down. For several nights his respiration became so labored that he was forced to rise and sit up for many hours in a chair. He took ipecac, an emetic commonly used for general complaints. When that did no good, he went to Dr. Lawrence in such distress that he said he would take whatever medicine Lawrence ordered without even reading the prescription. In addition to prescribing purges and a lighter diet, Lawrence called in a surgeon who drew twelve ounces of blood from Johnson's arm. He got a little sleep that afternoon in a chair.

That night, after lying in bed for an hour or two, he rose, and with the help of Francis, reopened the vein to draw out about ten more ounces of blood. But then they could not stop the flow. Levett was hurriedly sent for, and with his help they managed to stanch the bleeding. When Johnson wrote to Mrs. Thrale describing the incident to her, Henry Thrale became angered that Johnson had rashly put himself in such danger. "Master is very kind in being very angry," Johnson replied, "but he may spare his anger this time. I have done exactly as Dr. Lawrence ordered, and am much better at the expense of about thirty-six ounces of blood. . . . For a good cause I have six and thirty more."[43]

Besides caring for his own health and looking after the welfare of the other household members, Johnson soon took on a new responsibility. Mrs. Desmoulins, formerly Miss Swynfen, Tetty's old friend and fellow lodger, was currently living in Chelsea, deeply sunk in poverty. She had moved to Birmingham, about the time of Tetty's death, to marry the writing master at the Free Grammar School; he died four or five years later, leaving her with a daughter and two sons. She returned to London, where her prospects of earning a living seemed better, and for a time she worked at a machine for stamping crepe. Later, she kept a boarding school for children.

Johnson remained in touch with her during the years and knew of her distress. He actually had little affection for the woman, for her personality contained a large measure of meanness and petty spite, yet he felt obligated to assist her because of family and personal ties. She was, after all, the daughter of his own godfather for whom he was named, and he could not forget that Dr. Swynfen had contributed a small sum so that he could attend Pembroke College, Oxford, the same college that Dr. Swynfen had attended. But despite these obligations, Johnson's charitable disposition made him genuinely sympathetic to Mrs. Desmoulins's plight.

Johnson invited her to take refuge in his house. She accepted and brought along her daughter. The two of them lodged in the same room as Poll Carmichael, whose lawsuit was still pending in the courts. Mrs. Desmoulins's younger son, John, did not live under Johnson's roof, but he spent much time there, and Johnson used what influence he had to find him work. With Mrs. Williams too ill to stir much from her bed, Mrs. Desmoulins assumed management of the kitchen, though she was less efficient than Mrs. Williams had been. Besides room and board, Johnson gave Mrs. Desmoulins a weekly allowance of half a guinea, more than a twelfth of his pension. With the addition of these two people to Johnson's household, it brought the total number of full-time dependents to seven—Mrs. Desmoulins and her daughter, Francis and his wife, Mrs. Williams, Miss Carmichael, and Robert Levett.

Out of this group, Levett was perhaps the least troublesome. He was certainly the least expensive to keep. Johnson maintained that Levett was indebted to him for nothing more than shelter, part of a penny loaf of bread at breakfast, and an occasional dinner on a Sunday. Furthermore, Levett gave a good return for what he got, and Johnson considered himself fortunate to have so near a man "not solely a physician, a surgeon, or an apothecary, but all."[44] Though seventy-three years of age, Levett remained in excellent health and followed his profession diligently. He usually breakfasted with Johnson in the late morning or early afternoon, then left on his rounds of the poor tradesmen and their families who lived in and about Marylebone. He often did not return to Bolt Court till midnight. If Levett possessed any weakness or failing, it was that he sometimes returned home drunk, though Johnson admitted that he was perhaps the only man who ever became intoxicated through prudence. As his patients had little or no money, Levett collected his fees in whatever form they were tendered; often the fee was a drink of brandy or gin. Although he demanded nothing from those who could not pay, he declined nothing that was offered. "He would swallow what he did not like, nay, what he knew would injure him, rather than go home with an idea, that his skill had been exerted without recompence."[45]

It is difficult to think of two men more unalike than Samuel Johnson and Robert Levett. They had so little in common that people could not understand how they lived together so compatibly; yet when each man spoke of the other, it was in terms of respect and admiration. Sir John Hawkins was particularly perplexed. "Levett had not an understanding capable of comprehending the talents of Johnson," he said. "He had no learning, and consequently was an unfit companion for a learned man."[46] Johnson, on the other hand, was so inclined in Levett's favor that people thought he saw talents where none existed. Indeed, Johnson had so high a regard for his abilities, that he would hardly proceed in medical matters without first finding out Levett's opinion. "Such was Johnson's predilection for him, and fanciful estimation of his moderate abilities," said Boswell, "that I have heard him say he should not be satisfied, though attended by all the College of Physicians, unless he had Mr. Levet with him."[47] Summing up the general opinion of this odd relationship, Hawkins observed that "Levett admired Johnson because others admired him, and . . . Johnson loved Levett, because few others could find anything in him to love."[48]

All of this, of course, missed the point. What the men respected so much in the other was a tremendous capacity for charity. This was something many of the others lacked, so they could not understand its mutual attraction in men otherwise so different. Johnson saw it in Levett, though, and his admiration for a quality so rare did, perhaps, blind him to shortcomings elsewhere.

The household in Bolt Court, full of the destitute and needy, was the most prominent example of Johnson's beneficence. But while Levett understood intuitively and admired what he saw, Johnson's more respectable friends were merely puzzled; they could not fathom why Johnson saddled himself with such a varied and shabby crew. Some, like Frances Reynolds, Sir Joshua's sister, were more perceptive. Miss Reynolds recalled the favorable impression she had of Johnson the first time they met, when he told her that as he returned home at about one or two o'clock in the morning, "he often saw poor children asleep on thresholds and stalls, and that he used to put pennies into their hands to buy them a breakfast."[49]

Johnson was neither ostentatious nor falsely modest about such beneficence; he took it as a natural feature of his character. In his own estimation, it was his best trait. His diary often records sums of money given to "Girl at door," "To two Boys," "To poor Woman," "To the Soldier," "Poor man." He was conscious, furthermore, that acts of charity were acts of religion. He says in his *Idler*, No. 4, that charity, or "tenderness for the poor," is inseparable from piety, and he defines *piety* in his *Dictionary* as "discharge of duty to God." He might upbraid himself for his slothfulness, his lack of method in living, or his want of purpose in life, but he could not charge himself with want of tenderness for the poor. "In this last year," he wrote in his diary in the spring of 1779, "I have made little acquisition, I have scarcely read any thing. I maintain Mrs. Desmoulins and her daughter, other good of myself I know not where to find, except a little Charity."[50]

6 "Discord and discontent reign in my humble habitation as in the palaces of Monarchs."

Mrs. Williams continued much the same month after month, "very ill of a pituitous defluxion" as Johnson phrased it; in other words, she suffered a continuous discharge of phlegm and mucus, "which her physician declares himself unable to stop."[1] She went into the country for the summer months of 1777, Johnson having arranged comfortable lodgings for her in Kingston, "but, age and sickness, and pride, have made her so peevish that I was forced to bribe the maid to stay with her, by a secret stipulation of half a crown a week over her wages."[2] It was thought that the clearer air of the country might do her good, "but I have no great hope," Johnson declared. "I am afraid she can only linger a short time in a morbid state of weakness and pain.... we must all die: may we all be prepared!"[3] Writing from Edinburgh, Boswell commiserated over the poor woman's situation but told Johnson that at least he had the comfort of reflecting on his kindness to her. "Though her temper is unpleasant," he said, "she has always been polite and obliging to me." He further sent along a wish of many happy years to "good Mr. Levett, who I suppose holds his usual place at your breakfast-table."[4]

With the close of summer, Mrs. Williams returned to London and Johnson left for a stay in the Midlands. In September he received a letter from Mrs. Williams, written from dictation by one of her friends, saying that Dr. Lewis was attending her now that Dr. Lawrence had given up, and that Lewis had added ipecac to her daily medicine of an infusion of bark. Mrs. Desmoulins also wrote to him, but her letters seldom conveyed much information. Anxious to hear

71

about what was going on at home, Johnson asked Mrs. Thrale, in one
of his letters to her, if she knew anything of Bolt Court. "Dear Sir,"
she wrote from a shop in Dean Street, Soho,

> I have this Moment been at Bolt Court myself to pick up
> News such as you like: Mrs Des Moulines however wrote
> to you it seems two Days ago so now you know all without
> my help: Mr Levett was dusting Books, he hears Mrs Wil-
> liams mends a little under Dr. Lewis's Care—The fine
> Weather may also contribute something.[5]

Johnson wrote back saying that Mrs. Desmoulins had indeed
written, yet "I remember nothing in her letter, but that she was
discontented that I wrote only Madam to her, and dear Madam to
Mrs Williams. Without any great dearness in the comparison, Williams is I think, the dearer of the two."[6] He was pleased, however,
to learn that Mrs. Williams grew better, "but I am afraid she cannot
get the start of the season, and Winter will come before she is
prepared for it."[7]

Boswell again came to London in the spring. Mrs. Williams was
too ill to get around the house much, and Mrs. Desmoulins made
the tea, though tradition was preserved and it was drunk at Mrs.
Williams's bedside. Boswell declined, however, taking Easter dinner
with Johnson this year, "my stomach being so delicate that I could
not bear Mrs. Williams's cookery and *finger-feeding*."[8]

Fanny Burney, the twenty-six-year-old daughter of Johnson's
friend Dr. Charles Burney, the musical historian, had recently published her first novel, *Evelina*. It came out anonymously and enjoyed
a brisk sale. Only a few people knew of Miss Burney's authorship at
first, one of them being her close friend Mrs. Thrale. Though all in a
flutter over her book's reception, she was a shy and withdrawn young
woman, and she wished to conceal her identity from the curious and
prying eyes of the general public. She was alarmed, therefore, when
one day her maid handed her a note addressed to her father which
read,

> Mrs. Williams sends compliments to Dr. Burney, and begs
> he will intercede with Miss Burney to do her the favour to
> lend her the reading of *Evelina*.[9]

Although frightened that her anonymity might now be compromised, she was nevertheless pleased, for "Dr. Johnson must have spoken very well of the book, to have induced Mrs. Williams to send to our house for it."[10] She reasoned that Mrs. Thrale had told Johnson her secret, Johnson had told Mrs. Williams, and Mrs. Williams had told whoever had written the note for her. She did not then know Mrs. Williams, but Dr. Burney did, so she wrote to her father in town urging him to get in touch with Mrs. Williams and impress upon her Miss Burney's genuine desire to remain unknown. Dr. Burney called at Bolt Court in person to convey his daughter's message. Mrs. Williams promised to keep her secret and apologized for having taken the liberty of making the request in the first place. She explained that she was already acquainted with the first volume of the novel, though she was "dependent upon a lady's good nature and time for hearing any part of it," and she was very anxious to hear the rest; that is why she had written the note. "Your daughter," she told Dr. Burney, "is certainly the first writer, in that way, now living."[11]

Evidently Mrs. Thrale had not taken seriously Miss Burney's claims of wishing to remain anonymous and had never impressed the notion upon Johnson. Mrs. Thrale had, in fact, already told several other people of Fanny's novel, so that most of the Johnson circle were buzzing about it, eager to read the book and see what this shy and pretty young daughter of Dr. Burney could do. Johnson mentioned to Mrs. Thrale, in evident surprise, that even Francis wanted to read it.

Several weeks after receiving Mrs. Williams's note, Miss Burney spoke with Johnson at Streatham. Johnson told her a great deal about Mrs. Williams, made out a list of her works, and invited Miss Burney to visit them at Bolt Court. She did so about the beginning of 1779 and was fondly petted and praised by both. "My only fear," said Mrs. Williams in jest, "is lest she should put me in a book!"[12]

In late summer of 1778, Mrs. Williams again went into the country, returning in October better than she had been in some time; yet better health did little to sweeten her disposition. Her chief antagonist now was Mrs. Desmoulins, whose malicious nature turned everyone against her. Dr. Lawrence, with Mrs. Desmoulins in mind, said that Johnson observed the precept of the Gospel, for he "was kind to the unthankful and to the evil."[13]

Mrs. Desmoulins and Mrs. Williams constantly fought, making Johnson's life miserable. Even Levett, known for his retiring disposition, grew passionate at last over the perpetual turmoil within the household. He grew to despise Mrs. Desmoulins so much that he tried to talk Johnson into evicting her. "Levet is rather a friend to Williams," said Johnson, "because he hates Desmoulins more, a thing that he should hate more than Desmoulins is not to be found."[14] He summed up the relationship within the household by saying, "Mr Levet who thinks his ancient rights invaded, stands at bay, *fierce as ten furies*. Mrs. Williams growls and scolds, but Poll does not much flinch. . . . Williams hates every body. Levet hates Desmoulins and does not love Williams. Desmoulins hates them both. Poll loves none of them."[15]

The house sheltered not only the seven permanent members, but Johnson also allowed temporary lodgers to come in, usually literary people down on their luck and desperately needing a place to stay until their fortunes improved. Alexander Macbean, for instance, Johnson's old dictionary assistant, was staying at Bolt Court. He was very much impoverished, and Johnson sent round to friends asking for money to help Macbean out.[16] Soon afterward, Macbean entered the Charterhouse as a poor pensioner.

Such people constantly drifted in and out of the house so that Johnson himself hardly knew at any one time who was spending the night under his roof. In this way, Bolt Court housed such an odd assortment of people, many of them squabbling and bickering with one another, that Johnson's friends found the entire *ménage* an amusing subject of conversation. Even Johnson, attempting to keep some distance between himself and the chaos of his household, occasionally treated it with levity. During heated disputes he would sometimes act as a rooting section, cheering on the underdog. "Today Mrs Williams and Mrs Desmoulins had a scold," he wrote to Mrs. Thrale, "and Williams was going away, but I bid her *not turn tail*, and she came back, and rather got the upper hand."[17]

One evening at the Thrales', the topic of conversation turned to Johnson's household. Fanny Burney recorded in her journal that Johnson's account of the group, its adventures and absurdities, was highly diverting. Mrs. Thrale had already mentioned to her that Johnson's house was "quite filled and overrun with all sorts of strange creatures, whom he admits for mere charity. . . ."[18] During the conversation, Mrs. Thrale asked how Mrs. Williams liked all this tribe of people.

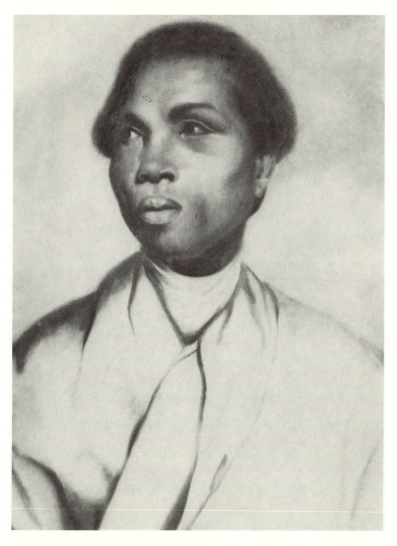

1. Francis Barber. Attributed to James Northcote. By permission of Dr. Johnson's House Trust, London.

Engraved by E. Finden.

2. Samuel Johnson at twenty-eight. From a miniature worn in a bracelet by Mrs. Johnson.

3. "Tetty" Johnson

MISCELLANIES

IN

PROSE AND VERSE.

By ANNA WILLIAMS.

LONDON:

Printed for T. DAVIES, in Great Ruſſel-Street, Covent-Garden.

M, DCC, LXVI.

4. From the first edition at The British Library, London.

5. Anna Williams. Attributed to Frances Reynolds, Sir Joshua's sister. By permission of Dr. Johnson's House Trust, London.

6. James Boswell. From the portrait by Sir Joshua Reynolds.

Engraved by F. ... ... final Painting

7. Mrs. Thrale

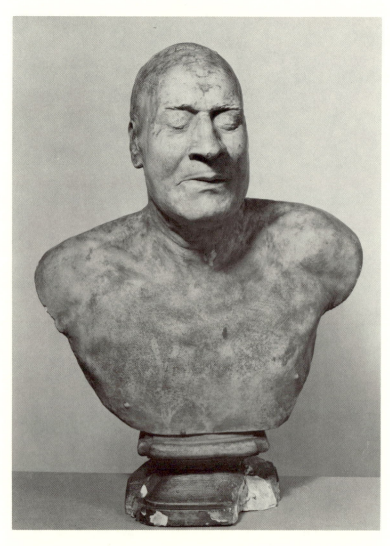

8. Death Mask of Samuel Johnson. By permission of the National Portrait Gallery, London.

"Madam," Johnson replied, "she does not like them at all; but their fondness for her is not greater. She and Desmoulins quarrel incessantly; but as they can both be occasionally of service to each other, and as neither of them have any other place to go .to, their animosity does not force them to separate."

Henry Thrale wanted to know who was clerk of the kitchen. "Why, sir, I am afraid there is none; a general anarchy prevails in my kitchen, as I am told by Mr. Levet, who says it is not now what it used to be."

"Mr. Levet, I suppose, sir, has the office of keeping the hospital in health?" asked Mrs. Thrale.

"Levet, madam, is a brutal [coarse] fellow, but I have a good regard for him; for his brutality is in his manners, not his mind."

"But how do you get your dinners drest?" asked Henry Thrale.

"Why, Desmoulins has the chief management of the kitchen; but our roasting is not magnificent, for we have no jack."

"No jack? Why, how do they manage without?"

"Small joints, I believe, they manage with a string, and larger are done at the tavern." Then assuming a look of profound gravity he said, "I have some thoughts of buying a jack, because I think a jack is some credit to a house."

"Well, but you'll have a spit, too?"

"No, sir, no; that would be superfluous; for we shall never use it; and if a jack is seen, a spit will be presumed."

Mrs. Thrale then asked, "But pray, sir, who is the Poll you talk of? She that you used to abet in her quarrels with Mrs. Williams, and call out, 'At her again, Poll! Never flinch, Poll'?"

"Why, I took to Poll very well at first," Johnson replied, "but she won't do upon a nearer examination."

"How came she among you?"

"Why, I don't rightly remember," said Johnson, perhaps wishing to avoid the subject of Poll's seamy origins, "but we could spare her very well from us. Poll is a stupid slut; I had some hopes of her at first; but when I talked to her tightly and closely, I could make nothing of her; she was wiggle-waggle, and I could never persuade her to be categorical." Turning to Fanny Burney, Johnson said, "I wish Miss Burney would come among us; if she would only give us a week, we should furnish her with ample materials for a new scene in her next work."[19]

It is little wonder, with all the squabbling, that Johnson lived more and more with the Thrales. He usually spent the middle of the week with them, either at Streatham in the summer or Southwark in the winter, and returned to Bolt Court on Saturday to check on his dependents and to see that they got three good meals over the weekend. On Monday evening he was usually back with the Thrales. Yet it was not just the squabbling that drove him out of his own house, but also the great attraction of the Thrale residences that *enticed* him out. Once out, however, he was loath to come back and face the complaints that had accumulated during the week.

He endured all of the complaints and the bickering not only because he felt sorry for the poor creatures under his care and wished to be charitable, but because, when it came down to it, he needed them as much as they needed him. They needed him for the necessities of life—food, shelter, and sometimes clothing. He needed them just to have someone around at all times. His horror of solitude was so great that having *anyone* around was preferable to being alone. Furthermore, he had many years before made a vow that when he talked, he would talk at his best. He kept strictly to that vow and always put great effort into his thought and conversation. The better known he became, the more often he found himself in the company of exceptional people who made the utmost demands on his powers. His mind could be more relaxed with the people whom he kept in his household, for they did not place such a burden on him to be brilliant; he enjoyed the luxury of having people about and not having to be at his best. He said in his most turgid style,

> The amusements and consolations of langour and depression are conferred by familiar and domestick companions, which can be visited or called at will, and can occasionally be quitted or dismissed, who do not obstruct accommodation by ceremony, or destroy indolence by awakening effort. Such society I [have] with Levet and Williams.[20]

After the first three-month stay at Streatham, in 1766, the Thrales reached an agreement with Johnson that he would spend at least half his time with them whenever both parties were in town. He had his own room at both Streatham and Southwark and always spoke of these places as home. His London cronies often felt annoyed that he stayed away so long. They complained among themselves that since getting to know the Thrales, Johnson seemed to have little time for them. Goldsmith wrote in his poem "The Haunch of Venison,"

> My friend bade me welcome, but struck me quite dumb,
> With tidings that Johnson, and Burke could not come.
> "And I knew it," he cry'd, "both eternally fail,
> The one at the House and the other with Thrale."[21]

Besides taking stray people into his house, Johnson sometimes took in stray animals. A black cat he called Hodge had been with him for years, slept in his room, and had the run of the house. "I am, unluckily," said Boswell, "one of those who have an antipathy to a cat, so that I am uneasy when in the room with one; and I own, I frequently suffered a good deal from this same Hodge." He recollected Hodge one day jumping up onto Johnson's breast, "apparently with much satisfaction, while my friend smiling and half-whistling, rubbed down his back, and pulled him by the tail." Boswell commented that Hodge was a fine cat. "Why yes, Sir, but I have had cats whom I liked better than this." But seeming to notice that Hodge was out of sorts, he added, "But he is a very fine cat, a very fine cat indeed."[22]

When Hodge at last grew so old and sick that he could eat nothing but oysters, Johnson went out to buy them himself so that Francis would not be offended by the chore and so take a dislike to the animal. After Hodge's death, Percival Stockdale, one of Johnson's friends, wrote a mock *Elegy on the Death of Dr. Johnson's Favourite Cat:*

> He lived in town, yet ne'er got drunk,
> Nor spent one farthing on a punk;
> He never filched a single groat,
> Nor bilked a taylor of a coat;
> His garb when first he drew his breath
> His dress through life, his shroud in death.
>
> . . . .
>
> Then in thy life exert the man,
> With moral deeds adorn the span;
> Let virtue in thy bosom lodge;
> Or wish thou hadst been born a Hodge.[23]

Hodge's place in the household was later filled by a white kitten named Lily.

In March of 1779, Johnson began publishing his *Lives of the English Poets*. Boswell had arranged for Francis to lay by and preserve for him the manuscript and proofsheets of the work. He wrote to Francis in January from Edinburgh reminding him of this, and Francis wrote back:

> Sir: I am extremely sorry, and also beg pardon for having put you to the necessity of writing, my engagement had not slip'd my memory but found it impracticable to collect the proof sheets regularly as they are work'd off; notwithstand the few which fell in my way I have carefully laid by in order to transmit them to you: however my Master has since order'd me to enform you that you shall shortly have the Books instead [sic] of the above sheets and am with due obedience, Your Humble Servant
>
> FRAS. BARBER[24]

Mrs. Williams's health declined a little during this time. Late in the summer she retired again to Kingston to see if clearer air would help her. Even with her absence, the wrangling in Johnson's house continued. "Mrs. Williams is not yet returned," Johnson wrote to Mrs. Thrale, "but discord and discontent reign in my humble habitation as in the palaces of Monarchs. Mr Levet and Mrs Desmoulins have vowed eternal hate. Levet is the more insidious, and wants me to turn her out."[25]

Mrs. Williams wrote to Johnson from Kingston saying that her health was still no better and that she had left off all medicines. Dr. Lewis, like Dr. Lawrence before him, had finally despaired of doing her any further good. She also informed Johnson that she would be returning to Bolt Court soon, to which he, anticipating the additional turmoil it would cause, remarked, "then there will be *merry doings.*"[26] Yet, surprisingly, after Mrs. Williams came back, a spell of relative quiet ensued, and Johnson informed Mrs. Thrale that "discord keeps her residence in this habitation, but she has for some time been silent. We have much malice, but no mischief."[27]

Mischief sprang up elsewhere, though. On 2 June 1780, anti-Catholic sentiment in London suddenly erupted into the infamous Gordon Riots. Lord George Gordon, Scottish member of Parliament and an influential member of the Protestant Association, organized a march on Parliament House where he presented a petition, containing 120,000 signatures, for repeal of the Catholic Relief Act of 1778.[28] This act legalized the purchase and inheritance of land by Catholics and also allowed them to enlist in the armed forces without renouncing their religion. The protestors, numbering about sixty thousand, were eventually dispersed by troops, but not before they had pummeled several ministers, destroyed their coaches, and burned down two Catholic chapels. Three days later, mobs looted other foreign chapels and burned several private homes.

On 6 June rioters broke into Newgate Gaol and freed the prisoners. From there some of them raided an arsenal, and after arming themselves, marched through the city pillaging and burning. The times were financially depressed, and joined to anti-Catholic feelings was a general distrust and hatred of the monied class; it was not hard for the rioters in their frenzy to link wealth with Popery, and several wealthy Protestants suffered from the mob's wrath as well as did many Catholics.

Rumor spread that Henry Thrale was a Papist, or at least a Catholic sympathizer, and some of the Newgate rioters made their way across the river to the Thrale brewery in Southwark. The Thrales were away at Bath, but Perkins, the superintendent, went out to meet the crowd. They were triumphantly dragging with them the great chains from the front of Newgate, and Perkins called out jocularly that it was a shame that *men* should be burdened with so heavy a load, and he offered to furnish them a horse for the purpose. He then welcomed them as guests, bringing out great quantities of meat and drink with which he hoped to pacify them. Meanwhile, a friend carried off the brewery's valuable papers to Chelsea College for safekeeping, then dashed in to town to summon troops. But it was Perkins's courage and presence of mind that saved the brewery from destruction, for the mob, having been pleasantly entertained, departed in high spirits amid a chorus of loud hurrahs.[29]

On 7 June, the following day, the rioters broke into other distilleries and burned more houses. The Lord Mayor had been reluctant to take any action to quell the disturbance, but the king finally called out the citizen militia. The mob launched an attack and the militia fired on them, killing twenty-two. Johnson was shocked by the sudden upheaval of violence in the capital and deplored the government's delay in moving to stop it. Mrs. Williams became so frightened that she fled by coach to the safety of her friends at Kingston.

Riots also broke out in Bath, where the Thrales were staying. On 9 June a crowd burned a new Catholic chapel there. The rumors of Thrale being a Papist had reached the town, and a report to that effect appeared in one of the local newspapers. Fearing for their lives, the Thrales left Bath the next day and headed for Brighton, traveling along country roads and avoiding big cities.

On the same day as the rioting at Bath, new violence flared up in London when mobs moved through the city burning and looting homes regardless of whether they were owned by Catholic or Protestant. Massed troops finally moved in and put down the rebellion, killing 285 and wounding 173. One hundred thirty-five rioters were arrested, and later twenty-one were hanged.

Mrs. Williams remained in the country until she was certain the violence had subsided. She finally returned to Bolt Court during the third week in July. She found her health a little improved, but now Mrs. Desmoulins was ill with a disorder "resembling an asthma." Johnson encouraged her to take calomel and jalop, both purgatives, but Levett followed a less drastic course in prescribing antimonial wine. Johnson's own health continued unstable; he was still plagued by difficulties in breathing, and he frequently suffered fits of colic. Levett, the oldest among them, was the only sound member of the household. Johnson mentioned in one of his letters to Mrs. Thrale, "If you want events here is Mr Levet just come in at fourscore [actually 75] from a walk to Hampstead, eight miles in August."[30]

A party was given as usual at the Thrales' country home of Streatham to celebrate the birthdays of Johnson and Queeney Thrale. Francis and Betsy made up part of the group free to enjoy themselves with dancing and other amusements. During the entertainment, some of the men servants made so bold as to flirt with Betsy. She did nothing to discourage them. Francis grew jealous, and in a fit of temper, he set out from Streatham to walk back to London alone. Mrs. Thrale and Johnson happened to be driving along the same road an hour later and overtook him. "What is the matter," asked Johnson, "that you leave Streatham to-day? Art sick?" Mrs. Thrale, who knew from her maids the nature of the trouble, whispered to him that Francis was jealous. Johnson could not tolerate sulkiness and bel-

lowed out, "Are you jealous of your wife, you stupid blockhead?"
Francis hardly knew how to respond to his master's angry outburst
and could only reply that he did not quite approve of the attentions
paid his wife by some of the footmen. "Why, what do they do to her,
man?" asked Johnson, "do the footmen kiss her?"

"No, Sir no!" stammered Francis. "Kiss my wife Sir! I hope not
Sir!"

"Why, what do they do to her, my lad?"

Francis confessed that they did nothing in particular. "Why then
go back directly and dance you dog, do; and let's hear no more of
such empty lamentations."[31]

By the end of the year, Mrs. Desmoulins had recovered from her
asthma. She still had no income, and she and her daughter continued
to be a drain on Johnson's purse. Johnson learned that the matron
of the boys school at the Charterhouse was soon to resign, and he
hoped that by pulling some strings he might get Mrs. Desmoulins
the position. He wrote to William Vyse, the rector of Lambeth, a
man whose father had known Mrs. Desmoulins' father in Lichfield.
Johnson wanted Vyse to mention Mrs. Desmoulins favorably to the
archbishop, who was to appoint the next matron. Mrs. Desmoulins
appeared qualified for the post, said Johnson, by having kept a boarding school for children, and furthermore, "She is in great distress,
and therefore may properly receive the benefit of a charitable foun-
dation."[32] Unfortunately for Johnson, who would have been pleased
to see Mrs. Desmoulins go, the archbishop chose someone else.

In addition to the turmoil that he had to suffer within his own
household, Johnson was further agitated when on 5 April 1781, Henry
Thrale experienced a severe stroke. He had suffered a previous stroke
in 1779, and from that time was plunged into the deepest depression.
His only relief seemed to be in travel and spirited company, but
these usually taxed his strength and left him in a state of deeper
gloom. Everyone perceived, however, that his greatest danger was in
overeating. His gluttony increased, and no one could dissuade him
from what appeared to be intentional suicide. On this particular
afternoon, when Thrale had put away so much food that "the very
Servants were frighted," Queeney went into her father's room and
found him lying on the floor, although conscious. "What's the meaning of this?" she asked with alarm.

"I chuse it," he replied firmly, "I lie so o'purpose."[33] Nevertheless, Queeney ran out to fetch Mrs. Thrale's servant. She told him to look after her father while she summoned help. As soon as the man entered the room, Thrale ordered him out, again saying that he chose to lie so. Finally, Sir Lucas Pepys, family friend and physician, arrived, but by then Thrale was in the throes of a violent apoplexy. Johnson was sent for late that evening and arrived near midnight. He found Thrale senseless and in strong convulsions. He sat by the bedside until Thrale died at about five o'clock the next morning. "I felt almost the last flutter of his pulse, and looked for the last time upon the face that for fifteen years had never been turned upon me but with respect or benignity."[34]

Mrs. Thrale, just forty years of age and inheriting a brewery with an annual profit of £30,000, was now a most eligible widow. It was only a matter of days before speculation began as to who would be her next husband. Johnson, so improbable a match in many ways, was deemed by many the front-running candidate because of his long and intimate association with the family. The prospect did not seem at all unlikely to Boswell, who was in London on his annual visit; in fact, he wished very much for it to happen. In a sportive mood, he went so far as to write, only eight days after Henry Thrale's death, a humorous and indelicate epithalamium in the style of Johnson, which, in its final version, he titled *Ode by Dr. Samuel Johnson to Mrs. Thrale upon Their Supposed Approaching Nuptials*. (See Appendix C.) Although he recited his *Ode* to a group of friends, including Sir Joshua Reynolds, two days after he wrote it, it was something he did not wish Johnson or Mrs. Thrale to hear about.

Despite the loss of his close friend, Johnson went ahead with his usual Easter dinner at Bolt Court. As he told Mrs. Thrale, "Our sorrow has different effects, you are withdrawn into solitude, and I am driven into company."[35] Boswell's stomach was not so tender this year as last, and he attended the feast. He saw that the members of Johnson's household lived together in greater disharmony than ever. Mrs. Williams was far more ill-tempered and Mrs. Desmoulins more spiteful. He noted that as Mrs. Williams talked, Mrs. Desmoulins would contradict and ridicule what she said while at the same time performing mocking gestures before her face.[36]

For this occasion, Johnson brought out the silver salvers he had bought years before. Seated at the table along with Boswell and the usual inmates were Mr. Allen, Johnson's landlord, Mr. Macbean, and

Mrs. Martha Hall, sister of John Wesley, founder of Methodism. Before them were soup, hashed veal's head, bacon-ham, fowls, broccoli, roast lamb, asparagus, pudding, porter, and port.

Mrs. Hall was a lean old woman with an exhortative manner of speaking in imitation of her brother. In answer to something Johnson said, she and Mrs. Williams began talking at the same time. Johnson, his nerves already frayed, cried out, "Nay, when you both speak at once, it is intolerable!" Then suddenly restraining himself, he added softly, "This one may say, though you are ladies." And to further lighten the mood, he quoted a line from *The Beggar's Opera*: "'But two at a time there's no mortal can bear.'"

"What, Sir, are you going to turn Captain Macheath?" asked Boswell, thoroughly amused by the entire scene.

"The term *ladies* applied to the two old animals was truly ludicrous," he later wrote in his journal. "And the contrast between Macheath, Polly, and Lucy, and Dr. Samuel Johnson, blind, peevish Mrs. Williams, and ancient, lean, preaching Mrs. Hall was exquisite."[37]

At about this time, Betsy Barber discovered she was pregnant. This created some stir, for Johnson was now persuaded that his servant's former display of jealousy might have been justified. This bred some apprehension that the child she carried was not her husband's. When the infant was born in the middle of November, Johnson was visiting friends in the Midlands, and accompanying him, rather than staying behind with his wife, was Francis. In a letter to Mrs. Thrale, Johnson wrote, "Frank's wife has brought him a wench; but I cannot yet get intelligence of her colour, and therefore have never told him how much depends upon it."[38] Two days later, having received no further news from Bolt Court, he wrote to his neighbor and landlord, Mr. Allen, saying, "I desire Mrs. Desmoulins to write immediately what she knows. I wish to be told about Frank's wife and child."[39] He eventually learned that the child, named Elizabeth, bore no Negro features. Whatever had been Frank's suspicions earlier, this discovery, in the words of Sir John Hawkins, "put an end to all his doubts on that score."[40]

7 "This little habitation is now but a melancholy place, clouded with the gloom of disease and death."

Dr. Johnson records in a letter to Bennet Langton[1] that he sat up late one winter's night, as he often did, musing. His thoughts turned for a moment to Robert Levett, his companion for more than thirty-five years, a man whom he valued not only for his knowledge of physic (perhaps more than it actually merited), but especially for the untiring diligence, humility, and humaneness of his character. Johnson vowed to himself that however his own mode of living might change or wherever he might move, he would do all in his power to keep Levett with him. He did not then consider how soon he might lose his friend, for Levett, despite his seventy-five years, continued in excellent health.

Yet the very next morning at about seven, a man who was sleeping in the same room with Levett, heard a strange noise from Levett's bed. He got up to investigate, and detecting something amiss, tried to make Levett speak. He could not; so he ran out to fetch the nearest apothecary, a Mr. Holder, who, on coming in, thought Levett dead, but he tried nevertheless to revive him by opening a vein; his suspicions were confirmed when he could get no blood to flow. Johnson was then staying with Mrs. Thrale in Harley Street where she had taken a house for three months at the beginning of the year. Francis carried the news of Levett's death to him there. He was naturally stunned by the unexpectedness of it; not a minute, it seemed, had passed between health and death. "So has ended the long life of a very useful, and very blameless man," he said. "How

93

much soever I valued him, I now wish that I had valued him more."[2]
Levett was buried three days later, on Sunday, 20 January 1782, between one and two o'clock in the afternoon in Bridewell's churchyard.[3]

Johnson commemorated his friend in the following verses, which
are thought to be among his best:

> Condemn'd to Hope's delusive mine,
>   As on we toil from day to day,
> By sudden blast or slow decline
>   Our social comforts drop away.
>
> Well try'd through many a varying year,
>   See Levett to the grave descend;
> Officious, innocent, sincere,
>   Of every friendless name the friend.
>
> Yet still he fills Affection's eye,
>   Obscurely wise, and coarsely kind;
> Nor, letter'd arrogance, deny
>   Thy praise to merit unrefin'd.
>
> When fainting Nature call'd for aid,
>   And hov'ring Death prepar'd the blow,
> His vigorous remedy display'd
>   The power of art without the show.
>
> In Misery's darkest caverns known,
>   His ready help was ever nigh,
> Where hopeless Anguish pour'd his groan,
>   And lonely Want retir'd to die.
>
> No summons mock'd by chill delay,
>   No petty gains disdain'd by pride;
> The modest wants of every day
>   The toil of every day supply'd.
>
> His virtues walk'd their narrow round,
>   Nor made a pause, nor left a void;
> And sure th' Eternal Master found
>   His single talent well employ'd.
>
> The busy day, the peaceful night,
>   Unfelt, uncounted, glided by;

His frame was firm, his powers were bright,
        Though now his eightieth year was nigh.

Then, with no throbs of fiery pain,
        No cold gradations of decay,
Death broke at once the vital chain,
        And freed his soul the nearest way.[4]

The house in Bolt Court was now a dismal place. What distressed Johnson most was its loneliness and lack of company. Levett
had been the only companionable member of the household for some
time. Francis no longer lived there. He had moved into rooms nearby
with his own family soon after his wife gave birth to her daughter.
He came to Johnson every day to perform his usual duties. Mrs.
Williams was wasting away by slow degrees, and Mrs. Desmoulins,
never affable anyway, was now also ill of a dropsy. "If I now go out I
must go far for company," lamented Johnson, "and at last come back
to two sick and discontented women, who can hardly talk, if they had
anything to say, and whose hatred of each other makes one great
exercise of their faculties."[5]

One of Johnson's few remaining pleasures was tending his garden. In the little plot of ground behind his house he had grapevines,
strawberries, and a fig tree for which he went one morning with
Boswell to a nearby ironmonger to buy a punch and a hundred nails
with which to nail up its drooping branches. Boswell noticed that
Johnson did not look well, and later he spoke confidentially to
Mrs. Williams about it. She told him that Johnson would not admit
that he had been ill once he got better, but when his complaints
returned again, he was very dreary. Boswell knew that Johnson had
not made out a will, and this concerned him. He told Mrs. Williams
that he ought to be spoken to on the matter. She thought that Boswell should do the talking. Boswell said that it was a delicate subject,
but that he would write to Johnson about it.

In May of 1783 the bickering with Mrs. Williams drove Mrs.
Desmoulins out of the house at last—that and an indictment issued
against her for debt. She hurriedly left Bolt Court, taking her daughter
along, and went into seclusion to avoid arrest. With her gone, peace
returned to the house, but her departure also deepened the pre-
vailing solitude. Poll Carmichael, her legal case never having come
to anything, had left the household some months before to be swal-

lowed up in the anonymity of the great metropolis; now Johnson had only Mrs. Williams to share his meals; yet her sickness prevented her from being the sociable companion she once had been. Johnson said to Mrs. Thrale that he hoped always to resist the "blàck dog" of depression, but that now he was deprived of almost all those who used to help him drive it away.

> When I rise [he said] my breakfast is solitary, the black dog waits to share it, from breakfast to dinner he continues barking.... Dinner with a sick woman you may venture to suppose not much better than solitary. After Dinner what remains but to count the clock, and hope for that sleep which I can scarce expect. Night comes at last, and some hours of restlessness and confusion bring me again to a day of solitude. What shall exclude the black dog from a habitation like this?[6]

At about three o'clock in the morning on 17 June, Johnson awoke with his breathing constricted; he got out of bed and moved to a chair. He had found that he could breathe more easily sitting up than lying down, so that often he got more sleep in chairs than in his bed. Suddenly he was seized by an overwhelming giddiness in which his mind became dazed and his sensations muddled. This confusion lasted for perhaps half a minute, and as it subsided, he grew frightened that his mind in some way had been affected; he quickly prayed to God to spare his understanding however He might afflict his body. He wrote this prayer out in Latin to satisfy himself that his mind was unimpaired, but he soon discovered that he could not speak and then realized that he had suffered a paralytic stroke.

He drank two drams of wine, believing this would stimulate his speech, and put his body into "violent motion" hoping, likewise, to actuate the vocal organs; but it did no good. In what he considered even then an odd state of apathy, he went back to bed and slept until it was light. Francis came in talking later in the morning and did not immediately understand his master's silent importunity to read the slip of paper that he thrust at him. This note, which Johnson had difficulty writing because his hand tended to form wrong letters, briefly explained the situation and instructed Francis to carry another note to his neighbor Mr. Allen, and then to fetch Dr. Heberden and Dr. Brocklesby, both physicians.

After examining Johnson, the doctors thought his recovery promising. By the same evening he had regained part of his speech. To hasten his cure, the doctors applied, as counterirritants, a blister to his back and one to each side of his neck from the ear to the throat. In addition, a preparation of dried beetles (cantharides) was spread liberally over his head. This was done for the same reason as application of the blisters—to produce a local and relatively superficial inflammation or blistering of the skin, theoretically reducing a deeper and more serious inflammation beneath. As is common with paralytic strokes, Johnson had a prolapse, in his case a slight distortion of the right corner of his mouth, though it nearly disappeared in two days as his powers of articulation improved. (This distortion of the mouth is clearly seen in Johnson's death mask.) He continued getting better, until several weeks after the stroke he could speak as clearly and distinctly as ever, though not so loudly or for so long a period of time, for his vocal organs quickly tired.

No sooner had he gained peace of mind about one disorder when another began troubling him. This disorder was actually of long standing, but whereas it had been a mere inconvenience before, it now flared up, threatening serious consequences. Two years earlier (sometime in the closing months of 1781), Johnson had noticed that his left testicle was appreciably larger than the right. It continued increasing in size, but it gave no pain or much inconvenience until the beginning of 1783 when, attaining the size of a hen's egg, it started hindering his walk. He thought it a hydrocele, or water swelling, and intended to have it drained as soon as he had sufficiently gained ground on the bronchitis and gout that afflicted him. The sudden stroke complicated matters and diverted his attention longer still. But finally in July, Mr. William Cruikshank and Dr. Percivall Pott examined Johnson and, at his request, attempted to drain the swollen testicle by puncturing it with a trocar; they found the ailment, however, not to be a hydrocele after all, but rather a more serious sarcocele, or swelling of the flesh itself. More time and greater thought was now required in determining what ought to be done.

Meanwhile, as Johnson struggled with the many ailments that seemed to be making ever greater inroads on his health, it became apparent that Mrs. Williams was sinking fast. "I am now broken with disease," Johnson wrote to Mrs. Thrale. "Levet is dead, and poor Williams is making haste to dye. I know not if she will ever more come out of her Chamber. I am now quite alone, but let me turn my thoughts another way."[7] Toward the end of August he wrote to Mrs. Thrale again:

> This has been a day of great emotion. The office of the Communion of the Sick, has been performed in poor Mrs. Williams's chamber. She was too weak to rise from her bed, and is therefore to be supposed unlikely to live much longer. She has, I hope, little violent pain, but is wearing out, by torpid inappetence and wearisome decay; but all the powers of her mind are in their full vigour, and when she has spirit enough for conversation, she possesses all the intellectual excellence that she ever had. Surely this is an instance of mercy much to be desired by a parting Soul. . . . The sense of my own diseases, and the sight of the world sinking round me, oppresses me perhaps too much. I hope that all these admonitions will not be vain, and that I shall learn to dye as dear Williams is dying, who was very cheerful before and after this aweful solemnity, and seems to resign herself with calmness and hope upon eternal Mercy.[8]

Through the month of August Mrs. Williams lingered on. Realizing that death was near, she gave £200 worth of stocks to The Ladies' Charity School, then made out her final will, leaving the school the remainder of her estate as well. But then her condition seemed to stabilize. She even fancied that she grew better, but Johnson knew this to be only a temporary remission. He did not believe, however, that she would die soon, and as he could be of little use to her, he decided to accept the invitation of the Reverend William Bowles, Canon of Salisbury, to spend some time with him at his estate of Heale.

Before leaving on Thursday, 28 August, he bid good-bye to Mrs. Williams in her room. The uncertainty of her health made it a more touching and emotional scene than it would ordinarily have been. Johnson asked her forgiveness for any misery he may have brought her. "I do not know that I have anything to forgive you," she told him. She assured him that she was fully prepared to die, adding simply, "I have set my house in order."[9]

Johnson went to Heale where he found the Bowles's estate handsome enough to "furnish without any help from fiction the scene of a romance."[10] He was treated with the utmost care and attention by his host and had everything he desired. A week after his arrival he received a letter from Dr. Brocklesby, and opening it, he read the news he so dreaded but half-expected. "Mrs. Williams, from mere inanition," wrote Brocklesby, "has at length paid the last debt to Nature, about 3 o'clock this morning (Sept. 6). She died without a struggle, retaining her faculties intire to the very last. . . ."[11] She was buried on the 12th and by her will, The Ladies' Charity School received all of her personal possessions and a little more than £157. (See Appendix D.)

Although Johnson enjoyed his stay at Heale, he was driven home at last by the sarcocele which had increased dramatically to about the size of a small orange. "Its weight," he said, "is such as to give great pain, when it is not suspended [i.e. supported by a truss], and its bulk such as the common dress does but ill conceal, nor is there any appearance that its growth will stop. It is so hot, that I am afraid it is in a state of perpetual inflammation."[12] He arrived at Bolt Court about noon on the 18th and stepped into an empty house. It was now, within the old familiar walls, once reverberating with the incessant bickering and quarrels of its inmates, and now so deathly still, that Johnson experienced the full impact of Mrs. Williams's absence. "Thirty years and more she had been my companion, and her death has left me very desolate."[13]

In the matter of the sarcocele there seemed little choice but to operate and remove the swollen testicle before it gangrened and spread infection to more vital organs. In this the doctors concurred, and the sooner the operation took place the better. Still, Johnson feared placing himself under the knife, for he dreaded not only the pain, but also the danger that any operation presented to a man of seventy-four years. Yet, in order to preserve his life, he was willing to risk it and was even eager to get the matter over with. The operation, however, had to be postponed when he was struck by a severe attack of gout, "with which in my present state, I did not care to play tricks."[14] The gout settled in his feet and ankles and rendered him nearly helpless; he could hardly raise himself in bed, "nor without much pain and difficulty by the help of two sticks convey myself to a chair."[15] But this was not all that he suffered. "To crown my other comforts," he said ironically, "a tooth tormented me. I was weary of being diseased from top to bottom; I therefore sent for a Dentist, and pulled it out."[16]

It was well the operation for the sarcocele had been postponed, for the puncture wound that had been made a month earlier in the testicle and then healed up, suddenly reopened, and over the next week discharged a great quantity of sanies, which diminished the swelling by at least half; it also lessened the pain to such a degree that the operation was suspended to see what more nature might do. The swelling continued decreasing until by November Johnson could say with great relief that "of the sarcocele I have now little but the memory."[17] The gout had also abated, and he claimed that his general health was better than for some years past.

Francis moved back in with Johnson, along with his wife and her child, and now that Mrs. Williams was dead, so did Mrs. Desmoulins, herself nearly incapacitated with a serious illness. But Johnson's own comparatively good health did not last long. In December he was again attacked by severe spells of asthma in which he struggled for breath, especially when lying down. "The asthma, however, is not the worst," he wrote to Boswell. "A dropsy gains ground upon me; my legs and thighs are very much swollen with water, which I should be content if I could keep there, but I am afraid that it will soon be higher. My nights are very sleepless and very tedious. And yet I am extremely afraid of dying."[18] He realized the dreadful significance of the dropsy, a condition in which watery fluids collect in serous cavities or in connective tissue. In a man his age it was generally fatal. But a surprising change took place late in February 1784 that Johnson considered almost miraculous; in the period of about twenty hours, with the help of vinegar of squills, a diuretic, he passed over twenty pints of liquid, considerably lessening the dropsical swellings. When Boswell came to London early in May, he found his friend in reasonably good health once again.

At Henry Thrale's death in 1781, Mrs. Thrale had taken charge of running the brewery. For some time afterward she was emotionally and temperamentally unsuited for such a heavy responsibility. Johnson had come to her assistance, proving himself a competent businessman. He fully enjoyed wrestling with bills and contracts, sometimes involving thousands of pounds in a single transaction. Mrs. Thrale, however, found it tedious and burdensome and soon determined that to preserve her health she must sell the business.

She and Johnson, therefore, negotiated with Perkins, the longtime, faithful superintendent of the brewery, and the brothers Robert and David Barclay, to sell the entire operation for £135,000, to be paid in four years. Being now free of the "Golden Millstone" as she called it, Mrs. Thrale, at the age of forty, again felt light and buoyant, able to "float once more on the Current of Life."[19] A great weight had been lifted from her—not only the weight of the Golden Millstone, but also the weight of many years having to play the role of "proper" wife to a successful London brewer and "proper" mother to his children. To a free spirit such as Mrs. Thrale, this had been the most oppressive weight of all. But now she felt suddenly giddy, light-headed, irresponsible, and with the return of her natural ebullience and girlish disposition, she discovered herself growing increasingly enamored of Queeney's music teacher, Gabriel Piozzi.

Piozzi had come from his native Italy in 1776 to London, where he gave concerts, singing in a pleasant tenor voice and playing the harpsichord or pianoforte. He also became a fashionable music teacher. Before Thrale's death, he had become a constant visitor at Streatham, not only instructing Queeney, but also furnishing the musical entertainments given there. He was handsome and charming, and contrasting him with her late husband, who had been reserved, cold, and unemotional, Mrs. Thrale found him excitingly warm, sensitive, and romantic. Her marriage to Thrale had admittedly been one of convenience on both sides, and while there had been respect and sometimes admiration, there had never been love; but now Piozzi began churning up emotions within Mrs. Thrale that she little knew she possessed.

Marriage with this man, of course, seemed out of the question. He was, after all, a foreigner who spoke halting English; he was a music master—not a prestigious calling in England; and he was a Catholic. But as their affection for one another deepened over the next year, Mrs. Thrale decided to toss caution aside and for once in her life look to her own happiness. Contrary to the advice of Fanny Burney and other close friends to suppress this foolish and unbecoming infatuation, and against the protests of her three daughters, led by her eldest, Queeney, she at last married her dear Piozzi.

She had not communicated her feelings or intentions about Piozzi to Johnson; in fact, she had not seen Johnson during the past year, flitting about as she did between Brighton and Bath, floating once more on the current of life, and avoiding Streatham with its depressing memories. The decision once made, however, she wrote to Johnson in June of 1784 begging his pardon

> for concealing from you a Connection which you must have heard of by many People, but I suppose never believed. Indeed, my dear Sir, it was concealed only to spare us both needless pain; I could not have borne to reject that Counsel it would have killed me to take; and I only tell it you now, because all is *irrevocably settled*, & out of your power to prevent.[20]

Johnson was furious. "God forgive your wickedness," he wrote to her, for it seemed that in marrying Piozzi she had abandoned her children, her country, her religion, and her honor. She wrote back, much hurt by Johnson's severity, defending her actions and her husband, whom she thought greatly wronged. She closed with the words, "till you have changed your Opinion of Mr. Piozzi—let us converse no more."[21]

Johnson wrote again, less passionate this time, but no less crushed, for in losing Mrs. Thrale to Gabriel Piozzi, he knew that the only link with the Thrale household, the place he considered home, the place representing the best period of his life, was forever severed. "What you have done," he wrote, "however I may lament it, I have no pretence to resent, as it has not been injurious to me. I therefore breathe out one sigh more of tenderness perhaps useless, but at least sincere.... The tears stand in my eyes."[22] Mrs. Thrale, now Mrs. Piozzi, wrote once more to Johnson before leaving with her husband for Italy, again defending Piozzi's respectability and wishing Johnson health. Not a word more ever passed between the two.

In June the asthma returned, persecuting Johnson's nights by sending him into painful coughing fits. It was accompanied the following month by a gradual return of the dropsy. On 6 July, no longer able to confide his miseries by letter to Mrs. Thrale, he began keeping a record of his illnesses, recording what medications he took and in what doses, and keeping track of the amount of his intake and elimination of liquids. He titled this diary AEGRI EPHEMERIS, or *Sick Man's Journal*. He fought a seesaw battle with the dropsy, his most dangerous ailment, and soon came to realize that he was losing;

"The dropsy encroaches by degrees," he recorded in his journal; "I felt this and today Frank told me of it."[23]

Johnson's very nature recoiled at the idea of his own dissolution; the thought of death terrified him. Still, he was practical, and he pondered what should become of Francis after he was gone. He asked Dr. Brocklesby what would be a proper annuity to leave a favorite servant, and Brocklesby responded that it largely depended on the circumstances of the master—a nobleman might leave £50 a year to a favorite servant for many years' service. "Then shall I be nobilissimus," replied Johnson, "for I mean to leave Frank £70 a year."[24] He told this to Francis, advising him that when the time came and he was on his own, he should move his family to Lichfield where his money would go further. Johnson knew that his servant was poor with finances, and although he planned to leave an annuity large enough to support him and his family comfortably if handled properly, he thought there would be less temptation to spend frivolously in a small town than in a great city.

Johnson spoke to Sir John Hawkins about making a will. Hawkins was a trained lawyer and could advise him on many of the details. But when Johnson mentioned his plans to provide for Francis, Hawkins protested the extravagant amount of the annuity and tried talking him out of it. Yet Johnson would hear no arguments. Except for this one point, Hawkins encouraged the idea of making a will, for he noted by the swelling of Johnson's legs the dreadful progress of the dropsy. Fearing the consequences, he urged Johnson to put his intentions into practice without delay. Yet the mere act of executing a will was abhorrent to Johnson; it seemed too much a concession to death, and so he kept putting off the business.

Hawkins, nevertheless, drew up a rough copy of a will, leaving blanks for Johnson to fill in with the names of people he wished to serve as his executors, blanks for the names of residuary legatees, and a space for him to direct how provisions of the will should be carried out. Johnson was about to leave in mid-July for a visit to Lichfield, Ashbourne, and Birmingham. Hawkins gave the draft to him just before he departed.

Johnson's health was now so much broken by the dropsy that he could hardly walk; any physical exertion caused him to pant and puff in asthmatic desperation to draw a breath. He entertained little hope of living much longer, and his trip was something of a farewell visit to the scenes of his boyhood and youth. Still, he was by no means giving in to his afflictions. "I will be conquered," he insisted, "I will not capitulate."[25] He fought his disorders with squills, opium, and diacodium, taking the medicines in such large quantities that he complained they sometimes made him comatose.

He remained in the Midlands nearly four months, but as his health deteriorated, he longed to be again in London. "The town is my element," he said, "there are my friends, there are my books to which I have not yet bidden farewell, and there are my amusements."[26] He returned to Bolt Court on 16 November 1784.

When Hawkins next called on him, he found that Johnson had done nothing in the matter of the will. Hawkins pressed him again, explaining the possibility of prolonged and ugly litigation among his relations should he die intestate. He added, furthermore, that Johnson had never mentioned to him how he wished the residue from his estate disposed of, which after providing Francis with an annuity, still amounted to a good deal. "I care not what becomes of the residue," said Johnson, irritated that Hawkins should pursue a subject so distasteful to him.[27] Several days later, however, he returned to Hawkins the rough draft, which he had signed as if it were a real will. Hawkins pointed out that he had not filled in the blanks. "You should have filled them up yourself," said Johnson.[28] Hawkins protested that it would appear to be tampering if he presumed to choose his executors for him. Johnson grumbled but finally promised to send for a clerk and dictate a proper will.

The dropsy, meanwhile, continued advancing, swelling his thighs and calves ever larger so that he now considered himself little more than a "bloated carcass," a "well of water." The asthma wracked him with painful fits of coughing, and he further noticed with alarm a return of the sarcocele. He asked Dr. Brocklesby if a puncture would not prove effective against this swelling as it had done a year before. Brocklesby said that it might, but that the best judge of that would be his surgeon, Mr. Cruikshank. Johnson put the question to Cruikshank and desired also that he make incisions in his legs to drain off some of the accumulating water. Cruikshank balked; he feared that in Johnson's weakened condition, such operations were too likely to gangrene. Johnson grew impatient with his faintheartedness and accused both him and Brocklesby of cowardice. "How many men in a year die through the timidity of those whom they consult for health! I want length of life, and you fear giving me pain, which I care not for."[29] Cruikshank finally relented, and to appease Johnson's demands, gently lanced the surface of his scrotum and thighs. "Deeper! Deeper!" urged Johnson. "I will abide the consequence: you are afraid of your reputation, but that is nothing to me. You all pretend to love me, but you do not love me so well as I myself do."[30]

In a calmer mood, Johnson asked Brocklesby how long he had left to live. "Give me a direct answer," he insisted. Brocklesby hesitated, then asked if he could bear the truth. When Johnson said that he could, Brocklesby estimated that he had but three to six weeks to live. "Then, I will take no more physick, not even my opiates; for I have prayed that I may render up my soul to God unclouded."[31]

On December 8th, Hawkins and Bennet Langton called at Bolt Court where they found Johnson dictating a will. In it he designated Hawkins, Sir Joshua Reynolds, and Dr. William Scott his executors. He left in trust to them £750 then in the possession of Bennet Langton; £300 then in the possession of Barclay and Perkins, the new owners of Thrale's brewery; £150 in the possession of Dr. Thomas Percy; £1,000 in 3 percent stock in the public funds; and £100 "now lying by me in ready money." From this total he directed that £200 be paid to the descendants of William Innys, bookseller in St. Paul's Churchyard, who had once assisted his bankrupt father, a bookseller of Lichfield. He further directed that £100 of the public funds stock be given Mrs. White, his female servant who did the washing and housecleaning. "The rest of the aforesaid sums of money and property, together with my books, plate, and household-furniture, I leave to the before-mentioned Sir Joshua Reynolds, Sir John Hawkins, and Dr. William Scott, also in trust, to be applied, after paying my debts, to the use of Francis Barber, my man-servant, a negro, in such manner as they shall judge most fit and available to his benefit."[32]

A codicil, dictated the following day, directed that further sums of money and certain books from his library be given as gifts to various friends, and that £100 be left with the Reverend John Methuen Rogers of Somerset, "requesting him to apply the same towards the maintenance of Elizabeth Herne, a lunatick," a first cousin once removed on his mother's side. The £750 in the hands of Bennet Langton was to be used in securing Francis his annuity. "All the rest, residue, and remainder of my estate and effects, I give and

bequeath to my said Executors, in trust for the said Francis Barber. . . ." Hawkins estimated that apart from the annuity, Francis
stood to gain from Johnson's estate about £1,500.

That evening Johnson was so weak and helpless that Hawkins
hired a man from the neighborhood at half a crown a night to sit
up and watch over him and administer to his needs till relieved by
Francis in the morning.

Fanny Burney called on the evening of the 10th. Francis let her
in, explaining that his master was very ill in bed upstairs. He offered
to take her up, but she would not go without Johnson's express desire
to see her. She told Francis not to disturb him, but say only that she
had called to pay her respects.

She came again after church the following morning, a Sunday,
and found the room outside his bedroom crowded with friends. Boswell was not among them. He was practicing law in Edinburgh. Francis told Miss Burney that Johnson was worse than yesterday and saw
no one.

By the 12th he had sunk even lower; his appetite was completely
gone, and he dozed most of the day. He was occasionally delirious.
At other times his mind was clear. He spoke with Hawkins and complained that the man hired to attend him at night was unfit for the
job. "He is an idiot, as aukward as a turnspit just put into the wheel,
and as sleepy as a dormouse."[33]

When Francis and Mrs. Desmoulins's son, John, visited Johnson
early on the morning of the 13th, they found him awake and alert.
He told Francis to open a cabinet and to give him a particular drawer
from it. The drawer contained a case of lancets. When Desmoulins
saw this, he objected to Francis handing the case over. "Don't you,
if you have any scruples," said Johnson, "but I will compel Frank."[34]
He ordered Francis to give him the case which Francis did reluctantly,
and from it Johnson selected one of the instruments and was about
to take it under the sheets when Francis and Desmoulins sprang
forward seizing his hand. "Scoundrel!" Johnson bellowed at Frank
and said that if Desmoulins did not let him go he would stab him.
They entreated him not to do anything rash, and when he promised
that he would not, they released his hand. Presently they saw move-
ment under the covers and quickly turned down the sheets to find
a pool of blood where he had cut himself in both the legs and the
scrotum. His desire for life was yet strong, and he was attempting

to gain more time by draining the dropsical swellings and the sarcocele. Fortunately, the wounds were not deep, and they soon stopped bleeding. Francis and Desmoulins confiscated the lancets, but later Johnson seized a pair of scissors from a drawer near the bed and plunged them deep into the calves of his legs. The other two hurriedly sent for Cruikshank and Mr. Holder, the apothecary, who dressed the jagged wounds. The loss of blood, about ten to twelve ounces, further weakened him, and about an hour later he fell into fitful dozing.

Francis and Mrs. Desmoulins sat with him for the rest of the day. During one of his lucid intervals, Mrs. Desmoulins asked for his blessing. "God bless you," he said weakly. Later in the day another woman earnestly sought his blessing; she was the daughter of Valentine Morris, one of Johnson's acquaintances. Francis led her from the street door up to Johnson's room and delivered her request. Johnson turned his head and replied, "God bless you, my dear."[35] Soon after, he lapsed into sleep and his breathing grew labored. At about a quarter past seven, Francis and Mrs. Desmoulins noticed that the noise he made in breathing had stopped. They went to his bedside and found that he was dead.

8 "Francis Barber is an exceedingly worthless fellow."

Two days after Johnson died, Dr. James Wilson performed an autopsy in the presence of Dr. Heberden, Dr. Brocklesby, Mr. Cruikshank, and others. It disclosed that Johnson had died from a number of causes—inflammation of the gallbladder, chronic emphysema, high blood pressure, chronic heart failure, and failure of the kidneys. (See Appendix E for Dr. Wilson's account of the autopsy.) He was buried in Westminster Abbey on the afternoon of 20 December, seven days after his death.

Sir John Hawkins became chief executor of Johnson's estate due to his legal background and his dedication to the duties at hand. He did not like Francis, and this influenced the manner in which he exercised his office in regards to him. It is difficult to say just when this dislike began, but the main reason for it lay in Frank's independent manner, which Hawkins took to be, in a black servant, gross impudence; Frank simply did not know his place. Frank's manner, of course, was largely of Johnson's fashioning, for Johnson had raised him from childhood, treating him with a fatherly regard and affection, attending to his intellectual and spiritual development, and taking an interest in the progress he made in the world. Francis was a servant pretty much in name only, for Johnson considered him a member of the household, on an equal footing with the other members. Indeed, Johnson, for all his love and support of Toryism and social hierarchy in the abstract, was, in practice, remarkably democratic.

Francis, however, became genuinely insolent toward Hawkins the more he dealt with the man, for he quickly perceived Sir John's unfriendly disposition toward him in administering the will. Only a few days after Johnson died, a relation of his, Humphrey Heely, came to Francis seeking money. Johnson had assisted him before. He lived with his second wife in an almshouse in Westminster and needed money to buy bedding and clothes. His claim on Johnson's benevolence through kinship was a slim one, for all it amounted to was that his first wife had been the daughter of Johnson's mother's brother. Yet Hawkins told Francis that since he had gained so much from Johnson's will, it was his duty "to have compassion on this his relation, and to supply his wants."[1] Thinking there might be no end to such importunities from distant and long-lost relations, Francis absolutely refused. He told Hawkins that he could not afford it.

A short time after, another request for money was made, this time in the name of Elizabeth Herne, Johnson's mentally ill cousin. She had been discharged from Bedlam Hospital some years before as incurable, and Johnson had placed her in a "madhouse" at Bethnal Green. Her upkeep was £25 a year. A little more than £10 was furnished by an annuity from a woman named Prowse. The remaining sum Johnson paid. Her bill was now £30 in arrears and the keeper of the madhouse applied to Hawkins for payment. Hawkins showed the bill to Francis who immediately went to the madhouse and tried to get the keeper to charge it to the legacy Johnson had left in his will to Mr. Rogers. The keeper refused. He said that Johnson had placed Miss Herne there himself, so that as the debt was incurred in his lifetime, it was payable from his estate. "When this would not do," Hawkins later recalled, "this artful fellow [Francis] came to me, and pretended that he could bring a woman to swear that there was nothing due; and, upon my telling him, that I should, notwithstanding, pay the bill, he said, he saw there was no good intended for him, and in anger left me."[2]

As chief executor, Hawkins retained in his possession Johnson's watch, some personal papers, some old coins, and a few other odd trinkets. He also had a gold headed cane that someone had left behind at Bolt Court shortly before Johnson's death and never reclaimed. The watch, apart from its having belonged to Johnson, was intrinsically valuable. It had been made especially for him in 1768 by Mudge and Dutton. It cost seventeen guineas. The outer case was covered with tortoiseshell, and the original dial plate had carried the inscription in Greek "for the night cometh." Three years later Johnson replaced the dial plate with a plain one as he thought the original ostentatious. By the terms of the will, these items now belonged to Francis, but Hawkins claimed them for himself as payment for the trouble he was put to as executor. He was perhaps legally within his rights to do so, but Francis complained to the other executors, Reynolds and Scott, who thought Sir John's actions a liberal interpretation of his rights. They finally persuaded him to surrender the watch, but they could not get back the other things. Hawkins later stated that the gold headed cane was lost in a fire at his house.

Francis journeyed to Lichfield shortly after Johnson's death hoping to find a house for his family. He brought with him Tetty Johnson's wedding ring which he intended to present to her daughter, Lucy Porter, but Mrs. Porter would not accept it, so when Francis returned to London having found no suitable residence, he had it enameled as a mourning ring for his wife in remembrance of his late master. Inside the band he had engraved "Saml Johnson L:L:D: OB: 13 Dec: 1784 AE. 75."

After this first half-hearted attempt to find a house in Lichfield, Francis remained with his family in London at No. 47 St. John Street, Smithfield. As Johnson had anticipated, Francis was careless with his money; it seemed to evaporate, he knew not where. He had greater responsibility, when, in 1785, his wife brought him a son, whom he baptized Samuel after his late master, but that did not account for the continual shortage of funds. In his distress, he frequently called upon Hawkins and the other executors for advances against his yearly annuity. Sir John's daughter, Laetitia Matilda Hawkins, recalled in her memoirs one of Frank's visits:

> I remember seeing him with all the vulgar insolence of a hackney-coachman, chuck up a few halfpence, which, he said, without rendering any reason, were all he had remaining of a large sum which he had received very shortly before, and urging Sir J. H. most indecorously to precipitation. . . .[3]

The executors always advanced him money when he asked for it, and by the first anniversary of Johnson's death, he had received £183. By the second anniversary of Johnson's death, he had received, apart from his annuity, £683.

The funds at last gave out in 1786. The executors had no more to give him. All that remained was the capital from which the £70 annual annuity was drawn. Only then did Francis move his family to Lichfield, about the month of September. They took a house in Stowe Street owned by Mrs. Gastrell, to whom they paid rent of twelve pounds a year. Mrs. Gastrell was the sister of Molly and Elizabeth Aston, all lifelong friends of Johnson. Hawkins was glad to be rid of Francis. He wrote to Bishop Percy saying, "Francis Barber is an exceedingly worthless fellow. He is gone to reside at Lichfield, and I have settled my account with him."[4]

Another reason why Francis may have moved his family to Lichfield at this particular time was to remove his attractive thirty-year-old wife from further temptations in London. Her first child, Elizabeth, had apparently not been Frank's. Little Samuel definitely was, for he resembled Frank in color and features. Not long after the family arrived at their new residence, a third child was born. She was baptized Ann in St. Chad's Church, Lichfield, on 7 November. Like her older sister, she possessed no Negro features, and people who saw her believed that she, too, was not Frank's.

Hawkins published his *Life of Samuel Johnson* early in 1787. He said many disparaging things in it about Francis and his wife. He thought the annuity Johnson had bequeathed to Francis a great mistake. Johnson had not been *nobilissimus* so much as foolish. Francis, for his part, was totally unworthy of the gesture. Betsy was an easy woman, "one of those creatures with whom in the disposal of themselves, no contrariety of colour is an obstacle," a strumpet who presented her husband "first with one, and afterwards with another daughter of her own colour."[5] Frank himself was a "loose fellow," stingy, uncharitable, and arrogant. Hawkins told of Frank's cold disinterest in the plight of Humphrey Heely and of his stinginess toward Elizabeth Herne, the insane cousin. He mentioned all this, he said, "as a caveat against ostentatious bounty, favour to negroes, and testamentary dispositions *in extremis.*"[6]

Many of Johnson's old friends thought Hawkins's book offensive, not for what it said about Francis, but because they felt it misrepresented Johnson. Reviewers found it tedious. One of them wrote, "A gentleman, lately arrived in town, has been for several days past afflicted with a *lethargy*, owing to the perusal of three chapters in Hawkins's *Life of Johnson.*"[7] Another said, "Sir John Hawkins—is to be *translated* into English: This is the work of Johnson's black footman. The motto, 'Hic Niger,' applying to Hawkins himself."[8]

Boswell, meanwhile, was putting together his own life of Johnson, but he was having trouble getting at the Johnson papers in Hawkins's possession. He did not know exactly what Hawkins had; perhaps there was nothing of biographical importance, but he was determined not to miss anything. Francis, being residuary legatee of Johnson's property, actually owned the papers. Boswell, therefore, wrote to Francis deploring the injurious statements Hawkins had made about him and his wife, and he expressed outrage over the injustice done to Johnson. "I cannot doubt of your inclination," he said, "to afford me all the helps you can to state the truth fairly, in the Work which I am now preparing for the press."[9] He wrote out a note authorizing himself to demand from Hawkins "all books or papers of any sort which belonged to the late Dr. Samuel Johnson."[10] He asked Francis to copy this note over in his own hand and return it to him.

Francis did as he was asked, and he also took the opportunity of enclosing another note requesting a loan of ten pounds. Boswell complied, sending him a bank post bill for the amount along with some words of advice couched in friendly language: "Some of your old Master's friends have thought that your opening a little shop for a few books and stationary [sic] wares in Lichfield might be a good thing for you."[11]

Upon Frank's authorization, Boswell obtained all the Johnson papers in Hawkins's possession. They did not amount to much. "There were but three pamphlets, the three diplomas of degrees from Dublin and Oxford, and a few papers for which I gave a receipt. . . ."[12]

Mrs. Desmoulins, after Johnson's death, had moved to the parish of St. Margaret's, Westminster, where her son and perhaps other friends cared for her. Her exact situation after leaving Bolt Court in 1784 cannot now be determined. She was close to seventy years old and, like Johnson, suffered from the dropsy. The records of St. Margaret's, Westminster, kept in the Muniments Room of Westminster Abbey, lists a burial for "Elizabeth Mouland" on 23 August 1786, which may not be she. We know, however, that she did not live past the spring of 1787, for in the Public Record Office can be found the grant of administration of her estate. This type of grant was made to the next of kin or principal creditor when a person had died without leaving a will. The grant of administration for Mrs. Desmoulins is dated May 1787:

Elizabeth Des Moulins On the twelfth day Admin of the Goods
Chattels and Credits of Elizabeth Des Moulins late of the
Parish of Saint Margaret Westm. in the County of Middx
Widow deced was granted to John Des Moulins the natural
and lawful Son and one of the next of kin of the said deced
having been first sworn duly to Adm. . . .

May 1787[13]

The Barbers were now well settled in at Lichfield, but the small
town did little to help them conserve money. They squandered it as
quickly in Lichfield as they had in London. For one thing, they tried
adopting a style to which they were unaccustomed and therefore
unable to manage. Samuel Barber, years later, said that his parents
"were improvident, strove to make a figure in the world, lived above
their means, and dissipated their property."[14] Although treated with
due respect by Johnson's old friends, who were the leading members
of the community, and although attempting to emulate their style of
living, Francis could never be accepted into their society; he was,
after all, a black servant. All he could do was make a show of high
living among the lower classes of the town to which he himself
belonged. Some of his new friends took advantage of his prodigality,
reducing his funds even more.

Other misfortunes also overtook him. He was only forty-eight
years old, but his health began declining rapidly. He suffered a return
of "my old complaint," perhaps the malady in his throat that troubled
him so much as a youngster. His eyes grew weak so that he could
hardly read or write. His wife fell dangerously ill, and all of his children came down with the smallpox. In the fall of 1790 he wrote a
frantic letter to Boswell:

Honoured Sir: It is with much Concern, and Feeling, I pen
these Lines, which I hope you will consider and pardon the
Liberty I have taken.

I wish I never had come to reside at this Place, but
being persuaded by my late poor dear worthy Master, to
whom I was, and ought, in duty bound, to oblige, was the
occasion. Some time ago, I was extreamly ill for a considerable time, which of course incurred a long Doctor's Bill,
which when I came to pay astonished me greatly at the
Total thereof, however I paid it: viz. 23.5.6, and some few

months prior thereto, I observe, I paid him, and another of the Faculty, upon Account of myself, my Wife and Family— 14 £. odd.

I have also been at a great Expence in the care an|d| Education of my Children, as it is my wish, upon my Master's Account to see them Scholars. . . .

As my Quarterly payment (as it becomes due) will not be sufficient to discharge the same and to leave me a farthing in Pocket to subsist upon, and having no friend here to assist me, or confide in; beg you will assist me in my distressed situation, and this a Neighbour of mine, a poor honest Man, advises me to do; if you would therefore be pleased to advance me 20 £. I will repay you honestly, by Eight Guineas on every my Quarterly days, with Interest, and for a further Security, will give you a Schedule of part of my household Goods, to such amount, in Case of Nonpayment, and this will be the means of Extricating myself from my present difficulties and put me streight |sic| into the world once again, and put my almost broken heart at reast |sic|, and for this kind and tender feeling Friend, from whom, 'till I hear, shall be very miserable. . . .

I have my Masters Diploma Box by me and several other Articles, if any of them you should like to have—shall be at your Command.

Francis Barber[15]

Francis had not paid back the ten pounds he borrowed from Boswell earlier, and he thought that if a simple appeal to his tender feelings did not move him to lend more, the offer to part with some Johnson relics might. Boswell wrote back saying that he was borrowing money himself and could not loan any. He reminded Francis by way of admonition that Johnson had been criticized strongly for having left him so large a provision. "It would be a sad thing," he noted to himself, "if the World should know that even that does not maintain him decently."[16]

Hard pressed, Francis turned elsewhere to find a market for some of the lesser Johnson items in his possession. Two months after his appeal for a loan, Anna Seward wrote to Boswell, saying, "I am afraid Poor Frank Barber has been very imprudent—that Doctor

Johnson's kindness has but little answered its purpose. I have given him three guineas for a carpet [of Johnson's] so worn, and thread bare, that it is not worth *one.*"[17]

Francis next began drawing upon the capital from which his annual seventy pounds income derived. Within three or four years that was gone and with it the annuity Johnson thought would secure his servant from want for the rest of his life. Then Francis began selling other Johnson relics. It had been merely diploma boxes and threadbare carpets before. Now he found it necessary to part with more valuable items. "O how will Boswell envy me!" wrote the Reverend Hugh Bailye, Canon of Lichfield, to his friend Richard Polwhele:

> No less than Dr. Johnson's watch is now in my possession! . . . I purchased it of Francis Barber, his black servant, who is now settled at Lichfield, and I am afraid in great want, though his master left him almost all his property. But he has a wife, poor fellow, that brings him both black and white children (alternately); this strange chemical mixture has produced that bitter portion poverty. This is not the Philosopher's stone.[18]

Francis was now fifty-one, yet his style of life, the worries it brought him, and his ill health had already made him an old man. He himself spoke of his ailments as the "infirmities attendant on age." A correspondent for the *Gentleman's Magazine*, passing through Lichfield in the summer of 1793, met with him and was struck by his premature decline. He wrote back to London, saying,

> Francis is 48 [*sic*], low of stature, marked with the small-pox, has lost his teeth, appears aged and infirm; clean and neat, but his cloaths the worse for wear; a green coat; his late master's cloaths all worn out. He spends his time in fishing, cultivating a few potatoes, and a little reading. He laments that he has lost the countenance and table of Miss S—— [Seward], and Mr. W——, and many other respectable good friends, through his own imprudence and low connexions.[19]

About four years later, some time before the year 1797, the Barbers moved to Burntwood, a hamlet four miles west of Lichfield, where Francis opened a school. Although never much of a scholar himself, he possessed enough education to help the village children with the rudiments of reading and writing. At his new occupation he made just enough to get by. Even so, as the years passed, his health grew so much worse that in 1800 he entered the infirmary at Stafford to undergo a painful operation from which he did not recover. He died the 13th of January 1801 aged fifty-nine. Two weeks later, on the 28th, he was buried at St. Mary's, Stafford.

Francis had been the youngest member of Johnson's household, and he survived the longest. His death came at the beginning of a new century and at the close of a period that his master in a large measure personified. Few of Johnson's intimate friends had lived so closely with the man who had given his name to an age. And not many of Johnson's friends could look back upon the old century and lament its passing: Hawkins had died in 1789, Boswell in 1795.

Betsy Barber continued on at Burntwood for a number of years following her husband's death. Elizabeth, the elder daughter, aged sixteen, who had long suffered from a persistent but unspecified ailment, died a year after Francis and was buried at St. Chad's Church, Lichfield, on 9 March 1802. Betsy moved back to Stowe Street in Lichfield and opened a daycare school for children that her daughter Ann helped her run for many years. Life was yet hard and money difficult to get. All that Francis had left her of value were a few Johnson items too personally dear to sell, but poverty forced her at last to part with them. She sold a tea service said to have been given Johnson by Warren Hastings, a bracelet once belonging to Tetty Johnson containing a miniature portrait of Johnson at age twenty-eight, and saddest of all, Tetty's wedding band that Francis had made over for her as a mourning ring.

Betsy survived her husband by fifteen years. She died at the age of sixty in Lichfield and was buried at St. Chad's Church on 8 April 1816.

Exactly what effect the household had on Johnson's writings is impossible to determine to any meaningful degree. The effect was more indirect and came from the significant role it played in his daily life. The household, for one thing, provided Johnson with ready recipients for his charity. He never had to look further than his own dwelling to discover unfortunate creatures in need of his care. And furnishing this care was the balm with which he tried to soothe a troubled mind that feared dissolution and doubted its own worthiness to receive mercy from that supreme benefactor, God. In providing for the present necessities of others, he also provided for the future needs of himself. Johnson wrote,

> What stronger incitement can any man require to a due consideration of the poor and needy than that the Lord will deliver him in the day of trouble; in that day when the shadow of death shall compass him about, and all the vanities of the world shall fade away. . . . In that dreadful hour shall the man whose care has been extended to the general happiness of mankind, whose charity has rescued sickness from the grave and poverty from the dungeon, . . . find favour in the sight of the great Author of society, and his recompense shall flow upon him from the fountain of mercy; he shall stand without fear on the brink of life and pass into eternity with an humble confidence of finding that mercy which he has never denied. His righteousness shall go before him and the glory of the Lord shall be his reward.[20]

The household, moreover, helped to allay Johnson's fear of madness. "Insanity," said Boswell, "was the object of his most dismal apprehension."[21] Madness resulted from an indulgent imagination, a preoccupation with "unpleasing ideas, . . . the remembrance of a loss, the fear of a calamity, or some other thought of greater horror," and nothing so much encouraged this morbid obsession as solitude.[22] "Solitude is dangerous to reason," said Johnson.[23] "Company in itself is better than solitude."[24] So he surrounded himself with persons whom he could always count on being there, and in this way the household lent stability to his life and allowed him the peace of mind to work.

Of the immediate Johnson circle, only Mrs. Piozzi lived long enough to see the blossoming of a new age in literature and to hear such fresh and unfamiliar names as Walter Scott and Lord Byron. She died in 1821. Judged by the critical attitudes of this new century, many of them antithetical to those of the old, Johnson's work proved its claim to a lasting place in English letters. And it was through the pages of Mrs. Piozzi's *Anecdotes*, Boswell's *Life*, and various other memoirs, that Samuel Johnson himself continued to live, lumbering down to our own day gruff and compassionate, wheezing and gesticulating, recognized as one of the great characters of literature; and never far from him is that odd assortment of unfortunate and impoverished souls, both a burden and a solace, who comprise his household.

Appendix A. Proposals for printing, by subscription, Essays in Verse and Prose, by Anna Williams

When a writer of my sex solicits the regard of the publick, some apology seems always to be expected; and it is, unhappily, too much in my power to satisfy this demand; since, how little soever I may be qualified, either by nature or study, for furnishing the world with literary entertainments, I have such motives for venturing my little performances into the light, as are sufficient to counterbalance the censure of arrogance, and to turn off my attention from threats of criticism. The world will, perhaps, be something softened, when it shall be known, that my intention was to have lived by means more suited to my ability, from which being now cut off by a total privation of sight, I have been persuaded to suffer such essays, as I had formerly written, to be collected and fitted, if they can be fitted, by the kindness of my friends, for the press. The candour of those that have already encouraged me, will, I hope, pardon the delays incident to a work which must be performed by other eyes and other hands; and censure may, surely, be content to spare the compositions of a woman, written for amusement, and published for necessity.

Appendix B.   To George Hay

Sir,
    I should not have easily prevailed upon myself to trouble a Person in your high station with a request, had I not observed that Men have commonly benevolence in proportion to their capacities, and that the most extensive minds are most open to solicitation.

    I had a Negro Boy named Francis Barber, given me by a Friend whom I much respect, and treated by me for some years with great tenderness. Being disgusted in the house he ran away to Sea, and was in the Summer on board the Ship stationed at Yarmouth to protect the fishery.

    It would be a great pleasure and some convenience to me, if the Lords of the Admiralty would be pleased to discharge him, which as he is no seaman, may be done with little injury to the King's service.

    You were pleased, Sir, to order his discharge in the spring at the request of Mr Wilkes, but I left London about that time and received no advantage from your favour. I therefore presume to entreat that you will repeat your order, and inform me how to cooperate with it so that it may be made effectual.

    I shall take the liberty of waiting at the Admiralty next Tuesday for your Answer. I hope my request is not such as it is necessary to refuse, and what it is not necessary to refuse, I doubt not but your humanity will dispose you to grant, even to one that can make no higher pretensions to your favour, than

    Sir Your most obedient and most humble servant

Grays Inn   Sam: Johnson
November the 9th 1759

Appendix C.   Epithalamium on Dr. J. and Mrs. T.

1

If e'er my fingers touch'd the lyre
In satire fierce or pleasure gay,
Shall not my Thralia's smiles inspire?
Shall Sam refuse the sportive lay?

2

My dearest darling, view your slave,
Behold him as your very Scrub,
Ready to write as author grave,
Or govern well the brewing tub.

3

To rich felicity thus rais'd
My bosom glows with amorous fire;
Porter no longer shall be prais'd;
'Tis I myself am Thrale's entire.

4

Piozzi once alarm'd my fears,
Till beauteous Mary's tragic fate
And Rizzio's tale dissolv'd in tears
My mistress, ere it was too late.

5

Indignant thought to English pride!
That any eye should ever see
Johnson one moment set aside
For Tweedledum and Tweedledee.

6

Desmoulins now may go her ways,
And poor blind Williams sing alone;
Levett exhaust his lungs in praise;
And Frank his master's fortunes own.

7

Congratulating crowds shall come
Our new-born happiness to hail,
Whether at ball, at rout, at drum;
Yet human spite we must bewail.

8

For though they come in pleasing guise,
And cry, "The wise deserve the fair!"
They look askance with envious eyes,
As the fiend looked at the first pair.

9

Ascetic now thy lover lives,
Nor dares to touch, nor dares to kiss;
Yet prurient fancy sometimes gives
A prelibation of our bliss.

10

From thee my mistress I obtain
A manumission from the power
Of lonely gloom, of fretful pain
Transported to the Blissful Bower.

11

Convuls'd in love's tumultuous throes,
We feel the aphrodisian spasm;
Tir'd nature must at last repose,
Then wit and wisdom fill the chasm.

12

Nor only are our limbs entwin'd,
And lip in rapture glued to lip;

Lock'd in embraces of the mind
Imagination's sweets we sip.

13

Five daughters by your former spouse
Shall match with nobles of the land;
The fruit of our more fervent vows
A pillar of the state shall stand!

14

Greater than Atlas was of yore,
A higher power to me is given;
The earth he on his shoulders bore,
I with my arms encircle Heaven!

(Taken from *Boswell: Laird of Auchinleck*, 1778–1782, ed. Joseph W. Reed and Frederick A. Pottle [New York: McGraw-Hill, 1977], 319–21.)

Appendix D.   Will of Anna Williams

In the Name of God Amen
I Anna Williams of Bolt Court Fleet Street in the Parish of Saint Dunstan in the West in the City of London spinster do declare this to be my last Will and Testament in manner and form following that is to say I give and bequeath to my Executrix hereinafter named all my personal Estate and Effects whatsoever In Trust after payment of my Debts and ffuneral Expenses to pay the Residue thereof to the Governesses or Trustees of the Ladies School institute for the Cloathing & Maintenance and Education of Girls now in or near the Parish of St. Sepulchres in the City of London aforesaid and I do hereby appoint Dorothy Owen of Tooks Court in the County of Middlesex Spinster to be Executrix of this my last Will and Testament hereby revoking all former Wills by me made In Witness whereof I have hereunto set my Hand this fourth Day of August in the Year of our Lord one Thousand seven Hundred and Eighty three. [signed] Anna Williams———/—/ Signed declared and published by the Testatrix Anna Williams the Day and Year above written in the Presence of us. [signed] Elizabeth Owen. James Wogan   Kings Remembrancers Office

This Will was proved at London the ffifteenth Day of September in the Year of our Lord one Thousand seven Hundred and Eighty three before the Worshipful George Harris Doctor of Laws Surrogate of the Right Worshipful Peter Calvert Doctor of Laws Master Keeper or Commissary of the Prorogative Court of Canterbury lawfully constituted by the Oath of Dorothy Owen spinster the sole Executrix named in the said Will to whom Administration was granted of all and singular the Goods Chattels and Credits of the deceased having been first sworn duly to administer etc.—

(Found in the Public Record Office, Chancery Lane, London.)

Appendix E. Asthma

Wednesday, December 15th, 1784: Opened the body of Dr. Samuel Johnson for Mr. Cruikshank, in the presence of Drs. Heberden, Brocklesby, Butter, Mr. C. and Mr. White. He died on Monday evening preceding. About a week before his death Mr. C. by desire of his physicians scarified his legs and scrotum, to let out the water which collected in the cellular membrane of those parts, Dr. Johnson being very impatient to have the water entirely gone. On the morning of the day on which he died he repeated the operation himself, and, cutting very deep, lost about ten ounces of blood; he used a lancet for this purpose; he was in too weak a state to survive such an apparently trifling loss. For several years past he had been troubled with asthma, for which he commonly used to take opium and found that nothing else was of any service to him; he had discontinued, however, this practice some years before he died.

On opening into the cavity of the chest, the lungs did not collapse as they usually do when air is admitted, but remained distended, as if they had lost the power of contraction; the air-cells on the surface of the lungs were also very enlarged; the right lobe adhered very strongly to the diaphragm; the internal surface of the trachea was somewhat inflamed; no water was found in the cavity of the thorax. The heart was exceedingly large and strong, the valves of the aorta were beginning to ossify; no more fluid than was common was contained in the pericardium. In the abdomen seemed to be incipient peritoneal inflammation and ascites; the liver and spleen were firm and hard; the spleen had almost the feel of cartlidge. A gall stone about the size of a pigeon's egg was taken out of the gall bladder; the omentum was exceedingly fat; nothing remarkable was found in the stomach; the folds of the jejunum adhered in several places to one another; there was also a strong adhesion by a long slip between the colon and the bladder; the pancreas was remarkably enlarged; the kidney of the left side tolerably good, some hydatids beginning to form on its surface; that of the right side was almost entirely destroyed, and two large hydatids formed in its place. Dr. Johnson never complained of any pain in this part; the left testicle was perfectly sound in structure, but had also a number of hydatids on its surface, containing a fatty gelatinous fluid, the right testicle had hydatids likewise, but the spermatic vein belonging to it was exceedingly enlarged and varicose. The cranium was not opened.

N.B. Mr. White, assisting me to sew up the body, pricked his finger with the needle; next morning he had red lines running up the arm, and a slight attack of fever.

(Taken from Russell Brain, "A Post-mortem on Dr. Johnson," in *Some Reflections on Genius* [Philadelphia: J. B. Lippincott, 1960], 99–100.)

Notes

Chapter 1

1. Except where otherwise indicated, the general information on Anna Williams, Zachariah Williams, John Harrison, and Stephen Gray is from the *Dictionary of National Biography*, 1937 edition.

2. John Pavin Phillips, "Mrs. Anna Williams," *Notes and Queries*, 31 May 1862, 421–22. In addition, Mr. Geoffrey Nicolle, local historian of Rosemarket, Wales, upon my request for information, has found the will of Zachariah's father, John, in the National Library of Wales. This document shows that John Williams was Vicar of Rosemarket from 1677 to his death in 1714. His wife was named Margaret. Two sons are mentioned. One is John, presumably the elder as he is mentioned first and is named after his father. John had three children: John, Richard, and Elizabeth. The second son is Zachariah, or "Zachery" as it is written in the will. Both sons were left five shillings. The vicar also left "To my grandchild Anna Williams one heyfer cald the browne heyfer goeing in three yeares," and to Anna's mother, Martha, "one cow cald the tulip cow."

3. See E. G. R. Taylor, "A Reward for the Longitude," *Mariner's Mirror* 45 (February 1959):59–66.

4. Zachariah Williams, *An Account of an Attempt to Ascertain the Longitude at Sea* (London: R. Dodsley and J. Jefferies, 1755), 2–4. Much of the information concerning Williams and his longitude scheme is from this article.

5. "A Description of Vaux-Hall Gardens," *Gentleman's Magazine* (August 1765):353–58; Christina Hole, *English Sports and Pastimes* (London: Batsford, 1949); and M. Dorothy George, "London and the Life of the Town," in *Johnson's England* (Oxford: Clarendon Press, 1933).

6. Zachariah Williams, *An Account*, 12.

7. Ibid., 15.

8. Walter Thornbury, *Old and New London: A Narrative of Its History, Its People, and Its Places* (London: Cassell, Peter & Galpin, n.d.), 2:380–404.

9. "Original Letters of Zachary Williams," *Gentleman's Magazine*, Supplement, 1787, 1158.

10. Ibid.

11. Many of the details concerning Zachariah's stay in the Charterhouse are from his account *A True Narrative Of certain Circumstances Relating to Zachariah*

Williams, *An aged and very infirm poor Brother Pensioner, in Sutton's Royal Hospital, The Charter-House* (London: 1749). Also see *Gentleman's Magazine*, Supplement, 1787, 1157–59.

12. "Nicholas Mann," *Dictionary of National Biography* (1937).

13. Anna Williams, "A Copy of the First Letter to Mr. *Mann*," 2; appended to Zachariah Williams, *A True Narrative*.

14. Ibid.

15. Anna Williams, "A Copy of the Second Letter to Mr. *Mann*," 6; appended to ibid.

16. "True Copies of the Letters Which were most humbly Addressed and Delivered to Lord Chancellor Hardwicke; and to Lord Chief Justice Willes: By their Lordships Most Obedient Humble Servant, Anna Williams"; appended to ibid.

17. "A True Copy of the Petition and Remonstrance of Zachariah Williams a Poor Pensioner in the Charter-House," 8; appended to ibid.

"Anna Williams, "True Copies of the Letters," 2.

18. Ibid., 5.

19. "We do Order that the said Ann Williams be forthwith Removed out of this House And that the Petitioner do not permit her to lodge or reside in his Apartment And that no payment shall be made to the Petitioner till he has Complyed with this Order And after he has complyed with this Order that the Master may make him the usuall Allowance to commence from the time of his complying with this Order and that a Copy of this Order be delivered to the Petitioner." A photocopy of this document was kindly supplied me from the Charterhouse records by Mr. J. Moss, Registrar and Clerk to the Governors.

20. From the Charterhouse records, furnished by Mr. Moss.

21. Zachariah Williams, *A True Narrative*, 14.

Chapter 2

1. Except where otherwise indicated, the information in this chapter on Johnson's early relationship with Anna and Zachariah Williams comes from John Nichols, *Literary Anecdotes of the Eighteenth Century* (London: Nichols, Son, and Bentley, 1812), 2:179–81; "Memoirs of Mrs. Anne [sic] Williams," *London Magazine* (December 1783):517–21; and "Original Letters of Zachary Williams; Some of them corrected, and others written, by Dr. Samuel Johnson," *Gentleman's Magazine* (September 1787):757–59 and Supplement 1787: 1041–59. Other information in this chapter, except where specifically noted, is from *Boswell's Life of Samuel Johnson*, ed. George Birkbeck Hill, rev. by L. F. Powell (Oxford: Clarendon Press, 1952).

2. See *Boswell's Life* 1:188–89; and James L. Clifford, *Dictionary Johnson: Samuel Johnson's Middle Years* (New York: McGraw-Hill, 1979), 46–51.

3. *The Letters of Samuel Johnson*, ed. R. W. Chapman (Oxford: Clarendon Press, 1952), 28.

4. See "Original Letters of Zachary Williams," 757–59 and Supplement 1787: 1041–42.

5. The information on Johnson's wife and on Henry Porter comes from various parts of Boswell's *Life*; various parts of Sir John Hawkins's *The Life of Samuel Johnson*, LL.D. (London: 1787); and from Hester Lynch Piozzi, *Anecdotes of the late Samuel Johnson, LL.D., during the last twenty years of his Life*, in *Johnsonian Miscellanies*, 1:248–49.

6. Boswell, *Life*, 1:238. Also see *Boswell: The Applause of the Jury, 1782– 1785*, ed. Irma S. Lustig and Frederick A. Pottle (New York: McGraw-Hill, 1981), 111, where Mrs. Desmoulins says that Mrs. Johnson "never had any love for him [Johnson] but [married him] only to get money from him" and that Mrs. Johnson "drank shockingly."

7. For Dr. Samuel Swynfen see Joseph Hill and Robert K. Dent, *Memorials of the Old Square* ([England]: n.p., 1897), 37–39; and various places in Boswell's *Life*.

8. Lustig and Pottle, *Boswell*, 111.

9. Ibid., 112.

10. See Hawkins's *Life*, 322–23.

11. Samuel Johnson, *The Rambler*, vol. 5 *The Yale Edition of the Complete Works of Samuel Johnson*, ed. W. J. Bate and Albrecht B. Strauss (New Haven: Yale University Press, 1979), 315–16.

12. Boswell, *Life*, 4:377, n. 1.

13. Ibid., 1:210.

14. Ibid., 238.

Chapter 3

1. Mary Manning Carley, *Jamaica: The Old and the New* (New York: Frederick A. Praeger, 1964), 34.

2. Robert F. Marx, *Pirate Port: The Story of the Sunken City of Port Royal* (Cleveland: The World Publishing Co., 1967), 80.

3. See W. J. Gardner, *A History of Jamaica* (London: T. Fisher Unwin, 1909), 101–51; and Carley, *Jamaica*, 44–46.

4. Carley, *Jamaica*, 39.

5. Gardner, *History of Jamaica*, 175.

6. Ibid., 135.

7. The information on the Bathursts in Jamaica comes from the *Dictionary of National Biography*, 1937 edition, and from records in The Jamaica Archives, Spanish Town, Jamaica.

8. Deed 137, 95, The Jamaica Archives, Spanish Town, Jamaica.

9. Deed 131, The Jamaica Archives, Spanish Town, Jamaica.

10. Boswell, *Life*, 1:239, n. 1.

11. Piozzi, *Anecdotes*, in *Johnsonian Miscellanies*, 1:158.

12. Boswell, *Life*, 1:144, no. 2. Information for the rest of this chapter, except where otherwise indicated, comes from Boswell's *Life* and from Hawkins's *Life*.

13. *Johnsonian Miscellanies*, 2:317.

14. Ibid., 1:12.

15. *Mrs.* in the eighteenth century did not signify only a married woman as it does today; it was also applied to unmarried women as a token of respect due usually to their age or abilities.

16. See *Diseases of the Lens and Vitreous; Glaucoma Hypotony*, Vol. 11 of *System of Ophthalmology*, ed. Sir Stewart Duk-Elder (St. Louis: The C. V. Mosby Co., 1969), 249–59.

17. *Philosophical Transactions, Giving Some Account of the Present Undertakings, Studies, and Labours, of the Ingenious, in Many Considerable Parts of the World*. Vol. XLVIII. *Part I. For the Year 1753* (London: C. Davis, 1754), 322–31.

18. *Gentleman's Magazine*, January 1754, 40.

19. T. C. Duncan Eaves and Ben D. Kimple, *Samuel Richardson: A Biography* (Oxford: Clarendon Press, 1971), 337.

20. Johnson, *Letters*, 51.1.

21. Boswell, *Life*, 1:280.

22. Ibid., 301–2.

23. Ibid., 274–75, n. 2.

24. Archibald Sparke, "Anna Williams," *Notes and Queries*, 8 September 1932, 198–99; and Nichols, *Literary Anecdotes*, 180.

25. As quoted by Lady Knight, "Mrs. Anna Williams," *European Magazine* 36 (October 1799):226.

26. The information on Francis Barber in the navy comes from Aleyn Lyell Read, *Francis Barber: The Doctor's Negro Servant*, Part 2 of *Johnsonian Gleanings* (London: privately printed, 1912).

27. Boswell, *Life*, 1:348.

28. Ibid., 348.

29. *The Letters of Tobias Smollett*, ed. Lewis M. Knapp (Oxford: Clarendon Press, 1970), 75, n. 5.

30. Ibid., 75.

Chapter 4

1. *Johnsonian Miscellanies*, 2:317.

2. Ibid., 1:306.

3. Boswell, *Life*, 1:328, n. 2.

4. The information on Robert Levett, except where otherwise indicated, is from Boswell's *Life*; the *Dictionary of National Biography* (1937); "Anecdotes of Mr. Levett, Dr. Johnson's Pensioner," in the *Gentleman's Magazine* (February 1785):101–2; Rev. James Foord, ed., *The Register of Kirk Ella, Co. York* (London: privately printed, 1897); and from a manuscript letter, in the Hyde collection at Somerville, New Jersey, from John Thompson to Samuel Johnson, dated 21 February 1782, a photocopy of which was kindly supplied me by Mary Hyde. Thompson's letter was in response to a letter from Johnson to Charles Patrick of Hull dated 14 February 1782, requesting information on Levett, who had died on 17 January 1782. See Johnson, *Letters*, 760.

5. See Sir D'Arcy Power, "Medicine," in *Johnson's England*, ed. A. S. Turberville (Oxford: Clarendon Press, 1933), 2:265–86.

6. Boswell, *Life*, 1:183.

7. Johnson, *Letters*, 130. For the information on Johnson at Staple Inn, see T. Cato Worsfold, *Staple Inn and Its Story* (London: Samuel Bagster and Sons, 1913), 102–5.

8. Boswell, *Life*, 1:421.

9. Johnson, *Letters*, 132.3.

10. The information on Francis Barber in the navy comes from Reade's *Francis Barber*.

11. John Nichols, *Illustrations of the Literary History of the Eighteenth Century* (London: J. B. Nichols and Son, 1831), 6:148.

12. Hawkins, *Life*, 414–15.

13. Nichols, *Illustrations*, 148.

14. *Johnsonian Miscellanies*, 1:416.

15. Boswell, *Life*, 1:331.

16. Ibid., 545.

17. Ibid., 322.

18. Ibid., 327.

19. Samuel Johnson, *Diaries, Prayers, and Annals*, ed. E. L. McAdam, Jr. (New Haven: Yale University Press, 1967), 75.

20. Arthur Murphy, "An Essay on the Life and Genius of Samuel Johnson, LL.D.," in *Johnsonian Miscellanies*, 1:408–9.

21. Ibid., 416.

22. Johnson, *Diaries*, 73.

23. Hawkins, *Life*, 382.

24. Boswell, *Life*, 1:374.

25. Ibid., 429.

26. Ibid., 1:429, n. 2.

27. Johnson, *Letters*, 142.

28. Ibid., 147.

29. Ibid., 150.

30. Boswell, *Life*, 3:26.

31. See ibid., 1:391–99.

32. Ibid., 436.

33. Johnson, *Diaries*, 77.

34. Boswell, *Life*, 1:397.

35. *Johnsonian Miscellanies*, 2:428.

36. See various places in Terence McLaughlin, *Dirt: Social History as Seen Through the Uses and Abuses of Dirt* (New York: Stein and Day, 1971); and also Clifford, *Dictionary Johnson*, 18–21.

37. Boswell, *Life*, 1:91, n. 1.

38. Ibid.

39. Samuel Pepys, *The Diary of Samuel Pepys* (20 October 1660), ed. Robert Latham and William Matthews (Berkeley: University of California Press, 1970–1983).

40. Boswell, *Life*, 1:399.
41. James Boswell, *Journal of a Tour to the Hebrides with Samuel Johnson* (19 July 1763), ed. Frederick A. Pottle (New York: McGraw-Hill, 1961).
42. Boswell, *Life*, 1:417.
43. Boswell, *Journal*, 2 August 1763.
44. Boswell, *Life*, 3:307.
45. *Johnsonian Miscellanies*, 1:241, n. 1.

Chapter 5

1. Boswell, *Life*, 1:496, n. 4.
2. Gillian Bebbington, *London Street Names* (London: Batsford, 1972), 185. The information in this chapter, except where specifically indicated, is from Boswell, *Life*, Hawkins, *Life*, and Piozzi, *Anecdotes*.
3. Johnson, *Diaries*, 103.
4. Johnson, *Letters*, 182.
5. Boswell, *Life*, 2:479.
6. As quoted by James L. Clifford, *Hester Lynch Piozzi* (Oxford: Clarendon Press, 1968), 61.
7. *Johnsonian Miscellanies*, 1: 234.
8. Ibid.
9. Boswell, *Life*, 1:483.
10. *Johnsonian Miscellanies*, 1:423.
11. Ibid., 234.
12. See various parts of Mary Hyde, *The Thrales of Streatham Park* (Cambridge: Harvard University Press, 1977).
13. Johnson, *Letters*, 207.
14. Reade, *Francis Barber*, 19.
15. Johnson, *Letters*, 238.
16. Boswell, *Journal*, 26 October 1769.
17. Boswell, *Life*, 2:99, n. 2.
18. *Plan of the Ladies' Charity School* (London: T. Bensley, 1805), 2.
19. Ibid., 3.
20. Ibid., 5.
21. Anna Williams, Letter to Anne Percy, 5 August 1772, The Hyde Collection, Somerville, New Jersey.
22. Piozzi, Hester Lynch Thrale, *Thraliana: The Diary of Mrs. Hester Lynch Thrale (Later Mrs. Piozzi) 1776–1809*, ed. Katharine C. Balderston (Oxford: Clarendon Press, 1951), 175; *Johnsonian Miscellanies*, 1:290–91.
23. Hawkins, *Life*, 328.
24. Boswell, *Life*, 2:215.
25. Johnson, *Letters*, 292.1.
26. Ibid., 293.1.
27. Boswell, *Journal*, 18 August 1773.
28. Nichols, *Literary Anecdotes*, 4:294 n.
29. Johnson, *Letters*, 361.

30. Boswell, *Journal*, 1 April 1775.
31. Johnson, *Letters*, 386.
32. Ibid., 390.
33. Ibid., 419.
34. Ibid., 422a.
35. Ibid., 427.
36. As quoted in John Wilson Croker's edition in one volume of Boswell's *Life* (London: 1847), p. 458.
37. Johnson, *Letters*, 472.
38. Ibid., 472.
39. Ibid., 502.
40. Ibid., 505.
41. *Johnsonian Miscellanies*, 1:291.
42. Johnson, *Letters*, 498.1.
43. Ibid., 351.
44. Hawkins, *Life*, 401.
45. Ibid., 399.
46. Ibid., 403–4.
47. Boswell, *Life*, 1:243.
48. Hawkins, *Life*, 404.
49. Frances Reynolds, "Recollections of Dr. Johnson," in *Johnsonian Miscellanies*, 2:250–51.
50. Boswell, *Life*, 3:380, n. 3.

Chapter 6

1. Johnson, *Letters*, 541. Information for this chapter, except where otherwise indicated, comes from Boswell's *Life*.
2. Ibid., 528.
3. Ibid., 524, 541.
4. Boswell, *Life*, 3:220.
5. Johnson, *Letters*, 551a.
6. Ibid., 553.
7. Ibid.
8. Boswell, *Journal*, 19 April 1778.
9. Burney, *Diary*, 3 August 1778.
10. Ibid.
11. Ibid.
12. Ibid., January 1779.
13. Boswell, *Life*, 1:83–84.
14. Johnson, *Letters*, 644.
15. Ibid., 590, 591.
16. See ibid., 394, 595.
17. Ibid., 586.
18. Burney, *Diary*, 1778.
19. Ibid.

20. Johnson, *Letters*, 921.
21. *The Vicar of Wakefield and Other Writings*, ed. Frederick W. Hilles (New York: Modern Library, 1955), 496.
22. Boswell, *Life*, 4:197.
23. Percival Stockdale, *An Elegy on the Death of Dr. Johnson's Favourite Cat* (New Haven: Yale University Press, 1949).
24. *The Correspondence and Other Papers of James Boswell Relating to the Making of the Life of Johnson*, ed. Marshall Waingrow (New York: McGraw-Hill, 1969), 15.
25. Johnson, *Letters*, 633.
26. Ibid., 640.
27. Ibid., 644.
28. For the Gordon Riots see Will Durant, *Rousseau and Revolution*, Vol. 10 of *The Story of Civilization* (New York: Simon and Schuster, 1967), 735–36.
29. For Perkins's part in saving the brewery see Piozzi, *Thraliana*, 437.
30. Johnson, *Letters*, 692.
31. *Johnsonian Miscellanies*, 1:291.
32. Johnson, *Letters*, 711.
33. Piozzi, *Thraliana*, 489.
34. Ibid., 489–90; Johnson, *Diaries*, 304.
35. Johnson, *Letters*, 719.
36. Boswell, *Journal*, 15 April 1781.
37. Ibid.
38. Johnson, *Letters*, 750.
39. Ibid., 751.
40. Hawkins, *Life*, 586.

Chapter 7

1. Johnson, *Letters*, 770.
2. Ibid., 770, 757.
3. The history of this churchyard is a lesson in the transience of all earthly things. L. F. Powell, in his revision of Hill's edition of Boswell's *Life*, says this:

> The Bridewell has had three churchyards in its long history; that in which Levett was buried was the third and last. The need for this new burial ground arose early in the seventeenth century, when a site adjacent to the chapel, at the bottom of Dorset Street and between it and Bridewell Place, was chosen; after great and for a time successful opposition from the Dorset family, whose mansion stood near by, a lease was obtained in 1680; this was renewed from time to time, till it expired in 1844, after which it was renewed annually till 1854, when the burial ground, which had never been consecrated, was closed by an order of the Home Secretary. The

land was then leased to a builder with the express stipulation that it was not to be built upon or disturbed in any way. It was subsequently bought by a firm of publishers and printers, who in 1901–3 promoted a Bill in Parliament to enable them to erect printing works on the site; the Corporation of the City and the London County Council joined the Governors in their opposition to this Bill, which was rejected by the House of Commons. The remains of many of those buried in the churchyard were removed to Ilford Cemetery in 1892–3 and 1903. The place is now [about 1934] a scene of forlorn untidiness and deplorable neglect. (4:498.)

I must add to this account that at as of 1984, the place where Levett was buried is the site of large office buildings.

    4. As quoted in Boswell, *Life*, 4:137–39. Except where otherwise indicated, the general information for this chapter comes from Boswell, *Life* and from Hawkins, *Life*.

    5. Johnson, *Letters*, 839.

    6. Ibid., 857.

    7. Ibid., 875.

    8. Ibid., 876.

    9. Johnson, *Diaries*, 366.

  10. Johnson, *Letters*, 879.1.

  11. Ibid., 880.

  12. Ibid., 874(1).

  13. Ibid., 884.

  14. Ibid., 888.1.

  15. Ibid.

  16. Ibid.

  17. Ibid., 906.

  18. Ibid., 932.

  19. Clifford, *Hester Lynch Piozzi*, 202.

  20. Johnson, *Letters*, 969a.

  21. Ibid., 970.1a.

  22. Ibid., 972.

  23. Johnson, *Diaries*, 403.

  24. Hawkins, *Life*, 581.

  25. Boswell, *Life*, 4:374.

  26. Johnson, *Letters*, 1029.

  27. Hawkins, *Life*, 576.

  28. Ibid., 579.

  29. Ibid., 585.

  30. Ibid., 589.

  31. Boswell, *Life*, 4:415.

  32. For the complete will see Hawkins, *Life*, 591–95.

  33. Ibid., 587.

  34. *Johnsonian Miscellanies*, 2:386.

  35. Boswell, *Life*, 4:417–18.

Chapter 8

1. Hawkins, *Life*, 596. The information for this chapter, except where otherwise indicated, comes from this source, from Boswell's *Life*, and from Reade, *Francis Barber*.

2. Hawkins, *Life*, 601.

3. Laetitia Matilda Hawkins, *Memoirs, Anecdotes, Facts, and Opinions* (London: Longmen, 1824), 1:153.

4. As quoted in Nichols, *Illustrations*, 8:244.

5. Hawkins, *Life*, 586.

6. Ibid., 602.

7. As quoted by Mary Hyde, *The Impossible Friendship* (London: Chato & Windus, 1973), 119.

8. Ibid., 119.

9. Boswell, *Correspondence*, 221–23.

10. Ibid.

11. Ibid., 278.

12. Ibid., 281.

13. Grant of Administration for Elizabeth Desmoulins, May 1787, Public Record Office, Chancery Lane, London.

14. As quoted by Reade, *Francis Barber*, 72.

15. Boswell, *Correspondence*, 335–37.

16. Ibid., 339.

17. Ibid., 337.

18. Rev. Richard Polwhele, *Traditions and Recollections; Domestic, Clerical, and Literary* (London: John Nichols and Son, 1826), 353.

19. *Gentleman's Magazine* (July 1793): 619–20.

20. George Birkbeck Hill, ed., *Wit and Wisdom of Samuel Johnson* (Oxford: Clarendon Press, 1888), 40–41.

21. Boswell, *Life*, 66.

22. Samuel Johnson, *The Rambler*, vol. 3 of *The Yale Edition of the Works of Samuel Johnson*, ed. W. J. Bate and Albrecht B. Strauss (New Haven: Yale University Press, 1979), 27–28.

23. *Johnsonian Miscellanies*, 1:219.

24. Johnson, *Letters*, 409.

Bibliography

PRIMARY SOURCES

Deed 131, Liber Old Series, between Richard Bathurst and Mark Hall. Entered 23 September 1747. The Jamaica Archives, Spanish Town, Jamaica.

Deed 137, Liber Old Series, between Richard Bathurst and William Lamb. Entered 30 September 1749. The Jamaica Archives, Spanish Town, Jamaica.

Grant of Administration for Elizabeth Desmoulins. May 1787. Public Record Office, Chancery Lane, London.

Orders issued by the governors of the Charterhouse relating to Anna and Zachariah Williams. Office of the Registrar and Clerk to the Governors, Charterhouse, London.

Thompson, John. Letter to Samuel Johnson, 21 February 1782. The Hyde Collection, Somerville, New Jersey.

Will of Anna Williams. Public Record Office, Chancery Lane, London.

Williams, Anna. Letter to Anne Percy, 5 August 1772. The Hyde Collection, Somerville, New Jersey.

———. Miscellanies in Prose and Verse. London: Tom Davies, 1766.

Wiliams, Zachariah. An Account of an Attempt to Ascertain the Longitude at Sea. London: R. Dodsley and J. Jefferies, 1755.

———. The Mariners Compass Compleated . . . . London: "printed for the author," 1740.

———. A True Narrative Of certain Circumstances Relating to Zachariah Williams, An aged and very infirm poor Brother Pensioner, in Sutton's Royal Hospital, The Charter-House. London: 1749.

SECONDARY SOURCES

Adam, Robert Borthwick. *The R. B. Adam Library Relating to Dr. Samuel Johnson and His Era.* Buffalo: privately printed, 1929.

Alkon, Paul Kent. *Samuel Johnson and Moral Discipline.* Evanston, Ill.: Northwestern University Press, 1967.

Balderston, Katharine C. "Johnson's Vile Melancholy." In *The Age of Johnson: Essays Presented to Chauncey Brewster Tinker.* New Haven: Yale University Press, 1949.

Bate, W. Jackson. *Samuel Johnson.* New York: Harcourt Brace Jovanovich, 1977.

Bebbington, Gillian. *London Street Names.* London: Batsford, 1972.

Boswell, James. *Boswell: The Applause of the Jury, 1782–1785.* Edited by Irma S. Lustig and Frederick A. Pottle. New York: McGraw-Hill, 1981.

————. *Boswell's Life of Johnson.* Edited by George Birkbeck Hill, and revised by L. F. Powell. Oxford: Clarendon Press, 1952.

————. *The Correspondence and Other Papers of James Boswell Relating to the Making of the Life of Johnson.* Edited by Marshall Waingrow. New York: McGraw-Hill, 1969.

————. *Journal of a Tour to the Hebrides with Samuel Johnson.* Edited by Frederick A. Pottle. New York: McGraw-Hill, 1961.

————. *The Life of Samuel Johnson, LL.D.* Edited by John Wilson Croker. One volume edition. London: 1847.

————. *The Yale Editions of the Private Papers of James Boswell.* New York: McGraw-Hill, 1950–1981.

Brain, Russell. *Some Reflections on Genius.* Philadelphia: J. P. Lippincott, 1960.

Burney, Frances. *Diary and Letters of Madame d'Arblay.* London: H. Colburn, 1842–1846.

Carley, Mary Manning. *Jamaica: The Old and the New.* New York: Frederick A. Praeger, 1964.

Chapin, Chester F. *The Religious Thought of Samuel Johnson.* Ann Arbor: University of Michigan Press, 1968.

Chaplin, Arnold. *Medicine in England During the Reign of George III.* London: privately printed, 1919.

Chapman, R. W. "Robert Levet." *Times Literary Supplement,* 1 January 1938, 12.

Clifford, James L. *Dictionary Johnson: Samuel Johnson's Middle Years.* New York: McGraw-Hill, 1979.

————. *Hester Lynch Piozzi.* Oxford: Clarendon Press, 1968.

"A Description of Vaux-Hall Gardens." *Gentleman's Magazine,* August 1765, 353–58.

Dictionary of National Biography. Edited by Sir Leslie Stephen and Sir Sidney Lee. Oxford: Oxford University Press, 1937.

Duk-Elder, Sir Stewart, ed. *Diseases of the Lens and Vitreous; Glaucoma and Hypotony.* Vol. 11 of *System of Ophthalmology.* St. Louis: The C. V. Mosby Co., 1969.

Durant, Will. *Rousseau and Revolution.* Vol. 10 of *The Story of Civilization.* New York: Simon and Schuster, 1967.

Eaves, T. C. Duncan, and Ben D. Kimpel. *Samuel Richardson: A Biography.* Oxford: Clarendon Press, 1971.

Emden, Cecil S. "Dr. Johnson's Ménage." *Quarterly Review* 649 (July 1966): 281–87.

Fleeman, J. D., introduction and notes. *The Sale Catalogue of Samuel Johnson's Library: A Facsimile Edition.* Victoria, B.C.: University of Victoria, 1975.

Foord, Rev. James, ed. *The Register of Kirk Ella, Co. York.* London: privately printed, 1897.

Gardner, W. J. *A History of Jamaica.* London: T. Fisher Unwin, 1909.

George, M. Dorothy. "London and the Life of the Town." In *Johnson's England.* Edited by A. S. Turberville. Oxford: Clarendon Press, 1933. Vol. 1, 160–96.

Goldsmith, Oliver. *The Vicar of Wakefield and Other Writings.* Edited by Frederick W. Hilles. New York: Modern Library, 1955.

Gow, A. S. F. "Dr. Johnson's Household." *Empire Review* 45 (January 1927): 23–32.

Grant, Lt. Col. F. *Life of Samuel Johnson.* 1887. Reprint, Port Washington, N.Y.: Kennikat Press, 1972.

Green, M. [i.e., John Nichols.] Letter to "Mr. Urban." *Gentleman's Magazine* 57 (July 1787): 557–59.

Hawkins, Laetitia Matilda. *Memoirs, Anecdotes, Facts, and Opinions, Collected and Preserved by Laetitia-Matilda Hawkins.* London: Longmen, 1824.

Hawkins, Sir John. *The Life of Samuel Johnson, LL.D.* London: 1787.

Hibbert, Christopher. *The Personal History of Samuel Johnson.* New York: Harper & Row, 1971.

Hill, George Birkbeck, ed. *Wit and Wisdom of Samuel Johnson*. Oxford: Clarendon Press, 1888.

Hill, Joseph and Robert K. Dent. *Memorials of the Old Square*. England: 1897.

Hilles, Frederick W., ed. *New Light on Dr. Johnson*. New Haven: Yale University Press, 1959.

Hodgart, M. J. C. *Samuel Johnson and his Times*. London: Batsford, 1962.

Hole, Christina. *English Sports and Pastimes*. London: Batsford, 1949.

Hopkins, Mary Alden. *Dr. Johnson's Lichfield*. New York: Hastings House, 1952.

Hyde, Mary. *The Impossible Friendship*. London: Chato & Windus, 1973.

————. "Tetty and Johnson." *Transactions of the Johnson Society*, December 1957, 34–46.

————. *The Thrales of Streatham Park*. Cambridge: Harvard University Press, 1977.

Johnson, Samuel. *Diaries, Prayers, and Annals*. Edited by E. L. McAdam, Jr. New Haven: Yale University Press, 1967.

————. *Johnson's Dictionary: A Modern Selection*. Edited by E. L. McAdam, Jr. and George Milne. New York: Pantheon Books, 1963.

————. *The Letters of Samuel Johnson*. Edited by R. W. Chapman. Oxford: Clarendon Press, 1952.

————. *The Rambler*. Edited by W. J. Bate and Albrecht B. Strauss. Vols. 3, 4, and 5 of *The Yale Edition of the Works of Samuel Johnson*. New Haven: Yale University Press, 1979.

Johnsonian Miscellanies. Edited by George Birkbeck Hill. 2 vols. Oxford: Clarendon Press, 1897.

[Knight, Lady Phillipina]. "Mrs. Anna Williams." *European Magazine* 36 (October 1799): 225–27.

Krutch, Joseph Wood. *Samuel Johnson*. New York: Henry Holt, 1945.

Letts, Malcolm. "Dr. Johnson's Cat." *Times Literary Supplement*, 7 November 1952, 732.

McHenry, Lawrence C., Jr. "Art and Medicine: Dr. Johnson's Dropsy." *Journal of the American Medical Association* 206 (9 December 1968): 2507–9.

Mackeith, R. "The Death Mask of Samuel Johnson." *New Rambler*, June 1968, 41–48.

McLaughlin, Terence. *Dirt: A Social History as Seen Through the Uses and Abuses of Dirt*. New York: Stein and Day, 1971.

Marshall, Dorothy. *Dr. Johnson's London*. New York: John Wiley & Sons, 1968.

Marx, Robert F. *Pirate Port: The Story of the Sunken City of Port Royal*. Cleveland: The World Publishing Co., 1967.

"Memoirs of Mrs. Anne [sic] Williams." *London Magazine*, December 1783, 517–21.

"Memoirs of Mr. Levet, with Dr. Johnson's Elegy on Him." *European Magazine* 7 (January 1785): 55–56.

Napier, Robina. *Johnsoniana: Anecdotes of the Late Samuel Johnson, LL.D.* London: George Bell and Sons, 1884.

Newton, A. Edward. "The Ghosts of Gough Square." In *The Greatest Book in the World*. Boston: Little, Brown, and Co., 1925.

Nichols, John. *Illustrations of the Literary History of the Eighteenth Century*. London: J. B. Nichols and Son, 1831.

———. *Literary Anecdotes of the Eighteenth Century*. London: Nichols, Son, and Bentley, 1812–1815.

O'Hara, James. "Frank Barber. Dr. Johnson's Black Servant." *Notes and Queries* 7 (3 July 1920): 13.

P., J. "William [sic] Levett." *British Medical Journal*, 11 April 1925, 705–6.

Pepys, Samuel. *The Diary of Samuel Pepys*. Edited by Robert Latham and William Matthews. Berkeley: University of California Press, 1970–1983.

Phillips, John Pavin. "Mrs. Anna Williams." *Notes and Queries*, 31 May 1862, 421–22.

Philosophical Transactions, Giving Some Account of the Present Undertakings, Studies, and Labours, of the Ingenious, in Many Considerable Parts of the World. Vol. XLVIII. Part I. For the Year 1753. London: C. Davis, 1754.

Piozzi, Hester Lynch Thrale. *Anecdotes of the late Samuel Johnson, LL.D., during the last twenty years of his Life*, in *Johnsonian Miscellanies*, vol. 1. Edited by George Birkbeck Hill. Oxford: Clarendon Press, 1897.

———. *Thraliana: The Diary of Mrs. Hester Lynch Thrale (Later Mrs. Piozzi) 1776–1809*. Edited by Katharine C. Balderston. Oxford: Clarendon Press, 1951.

Plan of the Ladies' Charity School. London: T. Bensley, 1805.

Polwhele, Rev. Richard. *Traditions and Recollections; Domestic, Clerical, and Literary*. London: John Nichols and Son, 1826.

Power, Sir D'Arcy. "Medicine." In *Johnson's England*. Edited by A. S. Turberville. Oxford: Clarendon Press, 1933. Vol. 2, 265–86.

Quinlan, Maurice J. *Samuel Johnson: A Layman's Religion*. Madison: University of Wisconsin Press, 1964.

Reade, Aleyn Lyell. *Francis Barber: The Doctor's Negro Servant*. Part 2 of *Johnsonian Gleanings*. London: privately printed, 1912.

————. "Francis Barber." *Times Literary Supplement*, 12 April 1934, 262.

Smollett, Tobias. *The Letters of Tobias Smollett*. Edited by Lewis M. Knapp. Oxford: Clarendon Press, 1970.

Sparke, Archibald. "Anna Williams." *Notes and Queries* 1 (8 September 1932), 198–99.

Stockdale, Percival. *An Elegy on the Death of Dr. Johnson's Favourite Cat*. New Haven: Yale University Press, 1949.

Taylor, E. G. R. "A Reward for the Longitude." *Mariner's Mirror* 45 (February 1959): 59–66; (November 1959): 339–41.

Thornbury, Walter. *Old and New London: A Narrative of Its History, Its People, and Its Places*. Vol. 2. London: Cassell, Peter & Galpin, n.d.

Verbeek, E., M.D. *The Measure and the Choice: A Pathographic Essay on Samuel Johnson*. Ghent, Belgium: E. Story Scienta, 1971.

W., T. S. "Notices of Dr. Johnson and Francis Barber." *European Magazine* 58 (October 1810): 275.

Wain, John. *Samuel Johnson*. New York: Viking, 1974.

[Waingrow, Marshall]. "Johnson's Degree Diploma." *Bodleian Library Record* 3 (December 1951): 238–39.

[Williams, Zachariah]. "Original Letters of Zachary Williams; Some of them corrected, and others written, by Dr. Samuel Johnson." *Gentleman's Magazine* (September 1787): 757–59, and Supplement 1787, 1041–42, 1157–59.

Worsford, T. Cato. *Staple Inn and Its Story*. London: Samuel Bagster and Sons, 1913.

Index